W9-DGD-579

Childhood Dialogues and the Lifting of Repression

Childhood Dialogues and the Lifting of Repression

Character Structure and Psychoanalytic Technique

Paul Graves Myerson, M.D.

YALE UNIVERSITY PRESS

NEW HAVEN AND LONDON

CARNEGIE LIBRARY
LIVINGSTONE COLLEGE
SALISBURY, NC 28144

Published with assistance from
the Mary Cady Tew Memorial Fund.

Designed by James J. Johnson and set in Trajanus types by
Keystone Typesetting, Inc., Orwigsburg, Pennsylvania.
Printed in the United States of America by Vail-Ballou Press, Binghamton,
New York.

Library of Congress Cataloging-in-Publication Data

Myerson, Paul G., 1914–
Childhood dialogues and the lifting of repression : character structure and psychoanalytic technique / Paul Graves Myerson.
p. cm.
Includes bibliographical references.
Includes index.
ISBN 0-300-04928-5 (alk. paper)
1. Psychoanalysis. 2. Parent and child. 3. Defense mechanisms (Psychology) in children. 4 Repression (Psychology) in children. I. Title.
[DNLM: 1. Child Development. 2. Parent-Child Relations. 3. Psychoanalytic Interpretation. 4. Repression. WM 460.7 M996c]
RC506.M94 1991
616.89'17—dc20
DNLM/DLC
for Library of Congress 90–13045
CIP

The paper in this book meets the guidelines for permanence and durability of the Committee on Production Guidelines for Book Longevity of the Council on Library Resources.

10 9 8 7 6 5 4 3 2 1

Contents

Introduction

In 1897 Freud concluded that instinctual conflicts, rather than traumatic events, are the precursors of neurotic syndromes.[1] This sudden shift in his understanding led to a profound change in the way the analysand is regarded in the analytic situation. A clinical approach based on the view that traumatic events are the source of the analysand's symptoms runs the risk of promoting the analysand's sense that he is a victim of external circumstances. It may sometimes be of value for an analysand to recover the memories of traumatic events and to re-experience the affects associated with them. In itself, however, this process does not allow the analysand to consider himself as the agent of his instinctual wishes. Under these circumstances, the analysand is likely to believe that the analyst concurs with his view that some external event or another person is responsible for what he is experiencing.

By contrast, an analyst who considers that instinctual conflicts play the more significant part in the genesis of psychopathology will perceive the analysand as having the potential to

1. Sigmund Freud (1914), On the History of the Psycho-Analytic Movement, in *The Standard Edition of the Complete Psychological Works of Sigmund Freud*, London: Hogarth Press (henceforth *S.E.*), vol. 14, pp. 17–19.

assume responsibility for his repressed wishes. The analyst endeavors to encourage the analysand to accept this responsibility by providing the analytic conditions under which the analysand will re-experience aspects of the wishes repressed early in life. This sense of responsibility develops when the analyst has succeeded in fostering the analysand's willingness to pay attention to whatever is taking place in his mind and to understand its significance. In this way, the analyst encourages the analysand to participate actively in the process of lifting the repression.

Freud viewed the lifting of repression as the fundamental and necessary outcome of a successful analysis. The analyst who conducts an analysis in accordance with Freud's classical approach regards it as a more critical aspect of the work accomplished through psychoanalysis than reality-testing or the modification of unrealistic expectations. Classical analysts may view the analysand's development of an increased ability to test reality or to modify expectations as a prerequisite for lifting repression or as a sequel to it. But they maintain that the analysand will benefit most from becoming aware of and learning to tolerate the repressed aspects of his instinctual wishes. This approach presupposes that the analysand's capacity to assume responsibility for his instinctual wishes is the aspect of the analytic work that brings about the resolution of his neurotic conflicts.

Although I am convinced that it is valuable for an analysand to assume responsibility for the archaic aspects of his libidinal and aggressive wishes, many analyses fall short of this goal. In the following chapters I shall address some of the reasons why this occurs. Sometimes it is because of the way the analyst conducts the analysis. He may not understand the intricacies of lifting repression, or he may not address in a helpful way the analysand's reluctance to accomplish the analytic work associated with it. This may be the case even when the analyst accepts Freud's premise that instinctual conflicts play the decisive role in the analysand's emotional difficulty.

Many analysands, moreover, do not have the potential for lifting repression. Obviously, an analysand who did not deploy repression as a significant defense during childhood is incapable of lifting it in the analytic situation. Throughout this book I make the assumption that only someone who has had helpful interactions and dialogues with a parent during his pre-oedipal and oedipal periods is capable of lifting repression. Such interactions and dialogues will have allowed him to deploy the sophisticated and selective defense of repression rather than the more global defenses of projection and denial. An analysand will be able to assume responsibility for archaic aspects of his instinctual wishes only if, as a child, he was helped to find a context for the less threatening aspects of his sexuality and aggression. I go on to assert that someone whose parents failed him in significant ways and who were not available to help him understand what he was experiencing will not develop the potential for lifting repression. He will be incapable of comprehending what his analyst expects him to accomplish. If the analyst insists upon conducting a classical analysis of such a person, the analysand can only feel misunderstood, and the analysis will not progress.

In recent years it has been widely maintained that for the analysand to lift repression and thereby to derive the greatest benefit from the analytic process, he must first experience his desire for and anger toward the analyst. It is generally held that the analysand who has experienced aspects of his instinctual wishes in the immediacy of the transference is likely to be convinced of their validity and therefore to accept responsibility for them. As early as 1909 Freud, discussing his treatment of the Rat Man, indicated how a "transference fantasy" allowed his analysand to experience "as though it were new and belonged to the present, the very episode from the past which he had forgotten, or which had passed through his mind unconsciously."[2] At that time, however, Freud considered that the crucial analytic work was accomplished once the analysand re-experienced the instinctual wishes of his childhood and assumed responsibility for them. Freud describes this process in the case of the Rat Man: "And so it was only along the painful road of transference that he was able to reach a conviction that his relation to his father really necessitated the postulation of this unconscious complement" (1909, p. 209). Freud argues that the analysand's transference interferes with his accomplishing the crucial analytic work: "Thus transference in the analytic therapy invariably appears to us in the first instance as the strongest weapon of the resistance."[3] Freud is maintaining that the analysand's unrecognized desire and anger toward the analyst may preclude his becoming involved in the work of lifting repression and thereby recovering his childhood wishes toward a parent.

James Strachey emphasized the importance of interpreting the analysand's transference in his often-quoted article "The Nature of the Therapeutic Action of Psychoanalysis."[4] Strachey does not view the recovery of childhood memories as the significant part of the analytic work. Accordingly, he does not consider transference to be a resistance to the work. Instead, he postulates that interpretation of the analysand's desire and anger toward the analyst, made at the correct time, will lead to "mutative changes." He indicates that the mutative effect of the interpretation is contingent on the analyst's offering it when the analysand is actually experiencing a feeling of desire or anger toward the analyst.

2. Sigmund Freud (1909), Notes upon a Case of Obsessional Neurosis, *S.E.* 10, p. 199.

3. Sigmund Freud (1912), The Dynamics of Transference, *S.E.* 12, p. 104.

4. James Strachey (1934), The Nature of the Therapeutic Action of Psychoanalysis, *International Journal of Psycho-Analysis* 15, pp. 127–159; reprinted in *Int. J. Psycho-Analysis* 50 (1969), pp. 275–292.

In this book I point to the conditions under which an analysand is motivated to respond favorably to any interpretation, whether it relates to his repressed feelings toward the analyst or toward events outside the transference. I am particularly concerned with the characteristics of the therapeutic relationship that must be present for the analysand to be willing to lift repression. It is true that interpreting transference reactions, in contrast to interpreting extratransference ones, calls the analysand's attention to feelings he is currently experiencing, and the immediacy of these feelings may help convince him of their validity. However, an analyst who interprets the feelings experienced in the transference is especially likely to be perceived by the analysand as critical of him. Regardless of whether the interpretations refer to the transference, the analyst must offer them in a manner that allows the analysand to realize that the analyst has his best interests in mind. The analysand is more likely to come to this realization if the analyst has explained the purpose of engaging in the analytic work and has been able to mitigate the analysand's concerns about his own involvement in it.

I shall call attention to the efforts the analyst makes to persuade the analysand to involve himself in the process of lifting repression. I stress those characteristics of the analytic dialogue that allow the analyst to define the type of analytic work he would like the analysand to accomplish and to alleviate the analysand's reluctance to do it. I believe that the analyst must promote the analysand's active involvement in the work in a manner that enhances the analysand's sense that he is cooperating, rather than complying, with the analyst. An analyst who attempts to overcome the analysand's reluctance to lift repression without addressing his concerns is apt to reinforce the analysand's resistance to the process. If the analysand has been intimidated by the analyst, he may go through the motions rather than participate actively in the analytic work. For an analysand to participate actively he must be helped to recognize the benefits of lifting repression.

Most descriptions of the therapeutic relationship in a classical analysis stress the importance of the analyst's maintaining a benevolent, if neutral, attitude toward his analysand. These descriptions fail to reveal the degree to which the analyst actively persuades the analysand to become involved in the analytic work. Freud indicates that if the analyst is not critical and does not take sides against the analysand, those aspects of the analysand's love for the analyst that Freud considers to represent an "unobjectionable" form of positive transference will motivate him to cooperate with the analyst (1912, p. 105). Freud's discussion of the conditions necessary for analytic work to be accomplished appears to focus on what the analyst should not do rather than on how he engages the analysand in the work. Freud's actual case material, however, shows that he actively attempted to persuade his analysands to participate in the process.

Strachey, like Freud, emphasizes the need for the analyst to relate to his analysand in a benevolent and helpful manner. He describes the analyst as "offering advice to the ego . . . consistently based upon real and interpersonal considerations" (Strachey [1934] 1969, pp. 281–282). Thus the analyst distinguishes himself from the way the analysand's parents had behaved toward him during his childhood. The analyst differentiates himself from the analysand's "too good" early objects, who had indulged him to his detriment, and from his "too bad" objects, who were overly critical of him. However, Strachey's formulation of the analytic process also largely ignores the extent to which the analyst actively persuades the analysand to become engaged.

Hans Loewald sees the parent-child relationship as the model for the analyst-analysand relationship: "The parent ideally is in an empathic relationship of understanding the child's particular stage of development, yet ahead in his vision of the child's future, and mediating this vision to the child in his dealings with him." Loewald maintains that "in analysis, if it is to be a process leading to structural changes, interactions of a comparable nature have to take place." He is suggesting that the child's "identification" with his parents' "vision of [his] future" is responsible for his healthy development.[5] A child's healthy maturation is undoubtedly promoted by his "identification" with, or perhaps more accurately his internalization of, the modes of behavior his parents suggest are in his best interest. In a classical analysis, however, where the aim is to help the analysand pay attention to his archaic wishes, the concept of identification and even the term *mediate* do not appear to take into consideration the active efforts the analyst must make to engage the analysand in the analytic work.

Ralph Greenson stresses the importance of the analyst's eliciting the analysand's active collaboration in the analytic work. He states, "Working through can begin only when the patient can simultaneously develop a working alliance with the analyst. Only then is the patient able to work along with the analyst when he makes his confrontations, clarifications, and interpretations. This means the patient can participate both actively and passively in trying to comprehend and associate to the analyst's interventions."[6] It is clear that Greenson considers it necessary for the analyst to play an active part in establishing a working alliance with the analysand. Most discussions of the therapeutic relationship do not sufficiently emphasize this need.

5. Hans Loewald (1960), On the Therapeutic Action of Psychoanalysis, *Int. J. Psycho-Analysis* 41, p. 20.

6. Ralph R. Greenson (1965), The Problem of Working Through, in *Essays in Honor of Marie Bonaparte*, ed. Max Schur, vol. 2, *Drives, Affects, Behavior*, New York: International Universities Press, p. 252; reprinted in Greenson (1978), *Explorations in Psychoanalysis*, New York: International Universities Press, p. 24.

In this book I contrast these analyst's attempts to encourage his analysand to participate in lifting repression with those in which the analyst insists that the analysand overcome his resistance and accept the analyst's ideas about the nature of his instinctual wishes. In practice, this distinction is somewhat difficult to make. Even when an analyst means to be encouraging, the analysand may feel he is insisting that the analysand accept his point of view. I suggest that an analyst is more likely to be perceived as encouraging rather than as insistent if he is alert to the inevitable concerns the analysand has about the analytic work. The analyst's awareness of the experiential aspects of these concerns will lead him to clarify them. These clarifications function as a form of encouragement and allow the analysand to risk engaging in the process of lifting repression. By contrast, the analyst who interprets his analysand's "resistance" to engage in the process as resulting from his unconscious instinctual conflicts is apt to intensify this resistance. It is one thing for the analyst to ascribe the analysand's reluctance to acknowledge his positive feelings for the analyst to his anxiety about whether the analyst will accept his feelings as valid; it is quite another for the analyst to interpret this reluctance as a manifestation of the analysand's wish to punish the analyst for not reciprocating his desire.

I maintain that only those individuals whose parents provided conditions favorable for deploying repression are capable of lifting it during psychoanalysis. It follows that an analyst will sometimes find it necessary to use an approach other than a classical one if he is to help an analysand whose childhood interactions forced him to deploy more primitive defenses than repression. The failure of the narcissistic analysand's parents to help him tolerate and understand what he experienced during childhood caused him to adopt the more global defenses of denial and projection instead of repression. It is therefore difficult for him to pay attention to and make sense out of the archaic aspects of his instinctual wishes evoked in the analytic situation.

A person with a marked narcissistic component to his personality is significantly impaired in his capacity to test reality as well as in his ability to lift repression. His difficulty in reality-testing keeps him from establishing intimate relationships with other people, a condition that has crucial implications for the analytic process.

Reality-testing is an important aspect of any analysis, whether it is conducted in a classical or in a nonclassical manner. Strachey notes that in a classical analysis the analyst's "advice" to his analysand is "consistently based upon real and interpersonal considerations." He suggests that an analyst who conducts a classical analysis not only engages the analysand in the process of lifting repression but also furthers his capacity to test reality. This allows the analysand to become aware of the distinction between the analyst's helpful attitude and the over-indulgent and critical ways in which his parents related to him in his childhood. The analysand's recognition of the analyst's real intentions toward him will allow him to trust the analyst as well as to promote his willingness to lift repression. I have suggested elsewhere that the classical analyst leads his analysand to a more realistic understanding of the relationship between various internal and external events.[7] This grounding in reality gives the analysand the security to focus attention on threatening archaic feelings.

A nonclassical analysis appears to be the best approach to treating a narcissistic analysand who has a more severe impairment in reality-testing than has a neurotic person. Accordingly, reality-testing is the major mode of intervention in a nonclassical analysis. However, delineating the process of reality-testing systematically is more difficult than delineating the process of

7. Paul G. Myerson (1981), The Nature of the Transactions That Enhance the Progressive Phases of a Psychoanalysis, *Int. J. Psycho-Analysis* 62, pp. 91–103.

lifting repression. This difficulty is largely due to the elusive nature of reality and especially to the fact that the analyst's view of the analysand's reality is shaped to a considerable extent by the perspective from which he examines it.

During his first analysis of Mr. Z, Heinz Kohut considered his analysand's mother to have behaved toward him naturally and affectionately.[8] He regarded the analysand's anger at her as a reaction to her rejection of his oedipal desire for her. But by the time of the second analysis Kohut's ideas about narcissism had evolved, and he now believed that Z's mother was using her son as an extension of herself and could not view him as an autonomous person. The mother's behavior had not changed, but Kohut's new way of understanding behavior led him to delineate it differently.

An analyst usually describes the process of reality-testing in general terms and does not indicate the aspect of his analysand's reality being evaluated or the extent to which his theoretical orientation influences the way he himself looks at this reality. The concept of reality-testing appears to be more difficult to piñ down than that of lifting repression, which culminates in the analysand's paying attention to and assuming responsibility for his own feelings. Although this outcome is often hard to achieve, the analysand does at least manage to observe his own inner somatic and mental activity—a more tangible type of observation than that directed toward external reality. Any notion of reality, even one acceptable to most observers, is shaped by factors whose presence may be deduced from their effects but that are not in themselves observable.

Classical analysts maintain that the primary goal of psychoanalysis is to lift repression. Their emphasis on the value of lifting repression partially explains why they have not devoted sufficient attention to the process of reality-testing. An analyst

8. Heinz Kohut (1979), The Two Analyses of Mr. Z, *Int. J. Psycho-Analysis* 60, pp. 3–28.

who holds steadfastly to the classical position will view adequate reality-testing as simply a secondary consequence of lifting repression. Such an analyst will believe that unless his analysand becomes aware of his archaic wishes, he will be incapable of modifying his unrealistic expectations and unable to recognize the effect of his behavior on others. It is my opinion that this point of view is seriously limited and certainly does not reflect how analyses, including most classical ones, are actually conducted. When we examine what takes place in the analytic situation, it becomes clear that many of the analyst's interventions directly concern reality-testing. Reality-testing is a significant aspect of the analytic work and has extremely important consequences for how the analysand will ultimately conduct his life.

Although little attention has been given to describing the analytic work associated with reality-testing, there has been considerable discussion of the kind of therapeutic relationship needed to bring about a change in the analysand's perception of reality. The self-psychologists make the case for establishing an empathic, nonconfrontational approach with the analysand. They believe that the analyst's willingness to mirror the analysand's view of himself and to allow the analysand to idealize him will enhance the analysand's self-esteem as well as his trust in the analyst. Under these conditions, they maintain, the analysand will be in a better position to formulate meaningful observations about his reality. They claim that the analyst must relate to the analysand in a manner that allows him to draw his own conclusions about reality. Quite correctly, they are cautioning against the possibility that the analyst will attempt to force the analysand to accept the analyst's conception of reality in place of his own.

This approach challenges the notion that the analyst's view of reality is more useful for the analysand than one he arrives at himself. The analyst may consider his own view of reality to have validity for himself, but it does not follow that it will be acceptable and useful to his analysand.

An analysand who as a child found it necessary to create his own version of reality to protect himself from the version his parents tried to force on him will be reluctant to accept his analyst's views about what is and is not real. The analyst who persists in his efforts to further the analysand's recognition that he has unrealistic expectations for himself and for his relationships runs the risk of intimidating him and forcing him to comply with the analyst's version of events. Even analysands who have had adequate childhood dialogues and are capable of lifting repression have a tendency to regard the analyst's interventions as criticisms. It is therefore likely that an analysand who has not had many helpful childhood dialogues will construe his analyst's clarifications of reality as a personal attack.

I argue that it is often necessary for the analyst to be persistent and, on occasion, somewhat insistent in his efforts to help a narcissistic analysand test reality. It has been my experience that many narcissistic analysands, even after their version of events has been mirrored by their analyst for a considerable period of time, remain oblivious to significant aspects of their reality. These analysands frequently regard the analyst's empathic stance as a clear indication that he is in complete agreement with their version of events. I believe that in this situation the analyst must be persuasive and confronting if he is to help him become more realistic. The analyst is faced with the issue of how best to confront a narcissistic analysand in a manner that does not intimidate and alienate him.

In his practice the psychoanalyst must often decide whether the analysand is capable of lifting repression. If he is, the analyst will use a classical approach. He will try to establish a therapeutic relationship that aims at helping the analysand assume responsibility for the archaic aspects of his instinctual wishes. When the analyst has determined that his analysand's early interactions have seriously limited his use of repression, the analyst must decide whether to switch from a classical approach to a nonclassical one. In those cases where a classical approach is not feasible, the analyst must decide how best to establish a therapeutic relationship and to determine what type of analytic work needs to be accomplished. In this book I will elaborate these issues so as to develop a more systematic view of the often bewildering and complex analytic situation.

1 Childhood Dialogues and the Nature of Analytic Work

Freud's definition of repression suggests that he viewed it as an intrapsychic process. He states, "Psycho-analytic observation of the transference neuroses . . . leads us to conclude that repression is not a defensive mechanism which is present from the very beginning, and that it cannot arise until a sharp cleavage has occurred between conscious and unconscious mental activity—*that the essence of repression lies simply in turning something away, and keeping it at a distance from the conscious.*"[1] This definition implies that one part of the mind is in conflict with another. A person's ego excludes from his awareness those aspects of his instinctual wishes that "cause pleasure in one place and unpleasure in another" (ibid.).

It is hard to take issue with Freud's definition. It has had a profound effect on the way psychoanalysts think about and practice their profession. Yet the definition does not focus on the important part one's interactions with other people play in the process. These interactions are significant both in childhood, when repression is deployed, and in the psychoanalytic situation, where it is lifted.

1. Sigmund Freud (1915), Repression, *S.E.* 14, p. 147.

Interpersonal transactions clearly have an essential role in the lifting of repression. During psychoanalysis the analyst's actions evoke both the analysand's repressed desire for him and his anger at him. In a classical psychoanalysis the analyst interprets to the analysand the significance of the feelings and fantasies emerging from repression. Inevitably, the analysand at first resists accepting these interpretations; it is hoped that later, after the analyst addresses these resistances, he will be able to respond favorably to them. Only at this point can lifting repression be construed as an intrapsychic process. A person who has been psychoanalyzed becomes aware of instinctual wishes he had previously kept at a distance, and as a consequence of his new awareness he may find more adequate ways of expressing his sexuality and aggression.

Although lifting repression in a psychoanalysis clearly involves the interaction of the two parties, it is less obvious that the deploying of repression in childhood is the outcome of interpersonal transactions. I have noted that repression is a much more sophisticated and selective mechanism than the more primitive defenses of denial, projection, and splitting. A child's relationship with his parents plays a crucial role in determining whether or not he deploys repression as his major defense. A child who has had a relationship with a relatively responsive parent during his pre-oedipal and oedipal periods deploys repression; one whose parents are in large measure unavailable is compelled to make use of more global and primitive defenses.

A person who deploys repression has the potential for lifting it in the psychoanalytic situation. Consideration of his analysands' relationships with their parents in childhood, particularly during the early years, helps the analyst decide which of them can make use of an analytic approach that has as its major aim the lifting of repression.

Obviously, it is not possible to know with any certainty the actual nature of the analysand's interchanges with his parents during childhood, but the analyst can infer something about the character of these early dialogues from the ways in which the analysand interacts with him, particularly on those occasions when the analyst offers a clarification or an interpretation. The analysand who displays genuine interest and tries to elaborate what has been suggested to him probably had relatively helpful exchanges with his parents. By contrast, the analysand who does not seem to integrate what has been pointed out to him probably did not have helpful childhood dialogues and was impelled to cope with his libidinal and aggressive feelings by making use of primitive defenses.

As the analysis progresses and the analysand's defenses are mitigated, the actual nature of the childhood dialogues becomes clearer. The analyst's approximate awareness of what occurred affords him a working hypothesis of the best approach to his clinical practice.

A look at the details of the childhood transactions through which repression is deployed may clarify some of the less obvious aspects of the analytic interactions essential for lifting it. The two situations are different in significant respects. The child ultimately turns his attention away from the more threatening and archaic aspects of his sexuality and anger. The analysand is encouraged to pay attention to and tolerate these same threatening elements of his instinctual wishes. Yet the two situations are similar in that the child and the analysand each need to recognize the helpful intention of the other party before he will be willing to use the sophisticated and selective mechanism of repression or lift it. In childhood, where repression is a leading mode of defense, the child perceives the parent as available to help him cope with certain aspects of his instinctual wishes. In psychoanalysis the analysand views the analyst as available to help him understand and tolerate those elements of his instinctual wishes that he had earlier repressed.

Of course, the child and the analysand perceive the parent and the analyst in quite different ways as well. Nonetheless, neither the child nor the analysand feels totally abandoned when he experiences his yearnings and anger, because both the parent and the analyst are alert to and attempt to mitigate his concerns about experiencing and expressing his libidinal and aggressive wishes.

A person whose parents were alert to his concerns about experiencing intense desire and anger as a child has the potential for responding favorably as an adult in a classical psychoanalysis. Such an analysand is capable of recognizing what the analyst expects him to accomplish when he encourages him to allow himself to lift repression. Sooner or later he will realize that the analyst is encouraging him to pay attention to the more archaic aspects of the desire and anger he has repressed.

Yet even an analysand with these favorable antecedents may be hesitant to respond to the analyst's encouragement to lift repression. He may be concerned that the analyst will not be available to help him tolerate his archaic sexuality and anger and understand what he is experiencing. He is likely to communicate this concern either directly or indirectly. When the analyst becomes aware of the analysand's concerns, he must attempt to allay them if the analysis is to progress. He may help the analysand clarify the nature of his concerns and recognize the unlikelihood that they are valid. If the analyst demonstrates to the analysand that he is alert to these concerns, that he is not critical of the analysand's hesitancy, and that he is making an effort to alleviate it, he is likely to convince the analysand that he will not be abandoned or criticized if he pays attention to what he is experiencing. Under these circumstances the analysand will perceive the analyst as helpful and will become less hesitant to play an active role in lifting repression.

There is, further, a parallel between the relatively helpful dialogue in childhood, as a result of which repression is employed, and the relatively helpful dialogue in a psychoanalysis, as a result of which repression is lifted. In both, the individual elaborates his feelings into the language of a fantasy, dream, or story, with the aim of either influencing the other person's behavior or obtaining his help in understanding himself. During the pre-oedipal and oedipal stages of development, the child invariably becomes troubled about the feelings of desire and anger he is experiencing toward his parents and siblings. If his relationship with his parents is reasonably good, he will try to let them know what he is experiencing. A significant purpose in elaborating his feelings into language is rhetorical, for he is attempting to persuade his parent to reciprocate his desire. When the child realizes that his desire is not reciprocated, he inevitably becomes angry. He may then tell his parent a fantasy, dream, or story to communicate his feeling. Here his purpose is more hostile, although he still may be trying to persuade the parent to renounce his rival (the other parent) and return his affection. The child's concern about how his parent might react to expressions of his desire and anger leads him to elaborate his fantasy in a disguised manner. Along with his effort to persuade his mother to reciprocate his desire, the child frequently appears to be asking her indirectly if she will still be available once she realizes the intensity of his feelings about her.

An alert parent who is not excessively threatened by the implications of the child's fantasy may attempt to help him make sense of what he is experiencing. Consider the interactions of a three-year-old child with his caring and available parents after he learned that his mother was pregnant. He told his mother a story about a young boy who took his sibling for a walk in the forest and lost him there. It is obvious that the child was indirectly letting his mother know he was angry at her and wished her to get rid of his unborn sibling. Equally significantly, however, the disguised expression of his anger in the fantasy toward his mother and unborn sibling indicates his concern about whether his mother would be tolerant and understanding of that anger. He was indirectly asking her whether she would remain available to him despite his angry feelings. The mother herself was concerned that if she did not try to help him find a useful perspective on his anger, he would believe that she no longer cared for him. To mitigate this unfortunate outcome, she let him know his reaction was understandable and natural. On several occasions when he repeated somewhat different versions of this fantasy, she told him that when she was a girl, she herself felt angry when her siblings were born.

This type of dialogue diminishes the child's sense of helplessness associated with experiencing feelings of intense desire and anger. Moreover, it sets the stage for the use of repression as his major defense. His mother's availability and responsiveness make it possible for him to remain actively engaged with her and to participate with her in furthering his understanding of himself. He anticipates that some kind of help will be forthcoming for coping with those aspects of his feelings that are likely to make him anxious.

Somewhat later in his development the deepening anxieties and threatening implications of his death wishes and incestuous yearnings make it essential for the child to turn his attention away from the more archaic aspects of his desire and anger. Nonetheless, if the parent continues to be accepting and helpful during this later period, the child will be encouraged to find ways of expressing the less primitive aspects of his instinctual wishes.

The significant consequence of the child's discovering that his mother remained tolerant and helpful during this dialogue is that his subsequent motivation for elaborating and reporting his dreams and fantasies becomes more complex and multidimensional. Even someone who uses his fantasies as a means of expressing his wish for gratification or his anger at not being gratified is simultaneously asking, in effect, whether the other party will remain available to him and will help him understand what he is experiencing.

The child who has been engaged in the kind of dialogue I am describing develops a capacity that later allows him to lift repression in the analytic situation. Such a person is capable of recognizing what the analyst is expecting him to accomplish when he offers him an interpretation. Under the appropriate circumstances he is willing to pay attention to his instinctual wishes. Although he inevitably has concerns and is hesitant to experience and pay attention to them, the propitious nature of his earlier interactions with his parent has enhanced his readiness to communicate his concerns to the analyst and to respond favorably when the analyst makes the effort to mitigate them.

Clearly, the analyst must be alert to his analysand's concerns and attempt to allay them if the analysand is to become willing to lift repression. Where the analyst is not alert to them, the analysis is likely to reach an impasse, which may persist until he addresses the analysand's hesitancy about paying attention to his feelings. This situation is distinct from that in which the analyst has failed to help the analysand realize that he needs to respond affectively before he can assimilate the meaning of the analyst's interpretations. The analyst who confines his interventions to "interpreting" that the analysand is angry at him for not reciprocating the analysand's desire may likewise find that the analysis has reached an impasse. To alleviate it, the analyst must convey to the analysand the importance of directing his attention toward his feelings.

In both of these situations there is a way for the analyst to provide the conditions necessary for conducting a classical analysis that aims at lifting repression. By contrast, there are times when it is necessary for the analyst to modify his approach greatly if he is to be of help to the analysand. Some persons have not had helpful dialogues with their parents in childhood and as a consequence do not deploy repression as a major mode of defense. In the analytic situation they are unable to recognize what type of work the analyst is expecting them to accomplish when he encourages them to lift repression. If the analyst attempts to implement a classical approach, such analysands will be confused, and the analyses will not progress.

The analyst conducting an analysis that has reached an impasse needs to consider whether he is using the wrong approach for the particular analysand or misemploying a correct approach. He must ask whether his intent to help his analysand lift repression is inappropriate because the analysand did not have the kinds of interactions in childhood that result in deploying repression as a major defense or whether the analyst himself has failed to provide the necessary conditions for his analysand to lift repression. It is obvious that this dichotomy does not address the full variety and complexity of human development or the many ways competent analysts conduct psychoanalysis. But by raising and addressing these questions, the analyst is in a better position to decide whether to modify his approach or try a new one.

This dichotomy is illustrated by Harry Guntrip's description of his own two analyses.[2] W. R. D. Fairbairn, Guntrip's first analyst, tried unsuccessfully to help lift repression of his instinctual wishes. Donald Winnicott, his second analyst, used an approach in which he accepted Guntrip's view that his mother was largely unavailable to him. According to Guntrip, Fairbairn had repeatedly emphasized oedipal issues:

> I developed a double resistance to him consciously, partly feeling he was my bad mother forcing her views on me, and partly openly disagreeing with him on genuine grounds. I

2. Harry Guntrip (1975), My Experience of Analysis with Fairbairn and Winnicott. *International Review of Psycho-Analysis* 2, pp. 145–156.

> began to insist that my real problem was not the bad relationships of the post-Percy period[3] but mother's basic "failure to relate at all" right from the start. I said that I felt oedipal analysis kept me marking time on the same spot, making me use bad relations as better than none at all, keeping them operative in my inner world as *a defense against the deeper schizoid problem.* (p. 147)

Although Guntrip felt that he had benefited from his analysis with Fairbairn, he believed that certain crucial issues had not been modified by this essentially interpretive approach. Consequently, he turned to Winnicott. His treatment with Winnicott consisted of 150 sessions over a period of six years. Afterward Guntrip wrote, "Winnicott said he was surprised that so much could be worked through in such widely spaced sessions, due I think in the first place to all the preliminary clearing that had been done by Fairbairn and to the fact that I could keep the analysis alive between visits; but most of all to *Winnicott's profound intuitive insights into the very infancy period I so needed to get down to*" (p. 152). Winnicott in general reaffirmed Guntrip's own ideas that his mother's early unavailability and failure had had a detrimental effect on his development, particularly compelling him to use extreme mental activity to ward off the state of emptiness that would otherwise have been his response to his lifeless mother.

Winnicott by and large did not use interpretation in his treatment of Guntrip or try to help Guntrip become aware of his conflicted wishes. Nonetheless, Guntrip reported that Winnicott would occasionally talk to him about "getting at [his] primitive sadism, the baby's ruthlessness and cruelty, [his] aggression" (p. 153). Guntrip felt that Winnicott was in this way suggesting that his anger at his mother was not only aimed at

3. Percy was Guntrip's younger brother, who died when Guntrip was three and a half years old.

extracting a response from a cold and unavailable person but in addition was related to "Freud's and Klein's instinct theory—the id innate aggression" (p. 153). At this point Winnicott was attempting to have Guntrip recognize that certain aspects of his anger were something other than a natural reaction to an unavailable mother. He was suggesting that Guntrip was angry at her because she, the object of his pre-oedipal and oedipal desires, did not reciprocate these desires and had turned her love elsewhere. Guntrip refused to accept this suggestion, which reminded him of Fairbairn's attempt to emphasize oedipal issues.

Significantly, Guntrip reports that Winnicott talked only occasionally about Guntrip's sadism. In particular, Winnicott did not encourage him to pay attention to the anger he experienced when his love for someone else was not reciprocated. It is likely that Winnicott believed that the vicissitudes of Guntrip's early development precluded him from making use of an interpretive approach. Perhaps he thought that if an analyst offered Guntrip any version of his past that differed from his own version, he would respond to him as if he were a "bad mother." In any case, Guntrip clearly did not accept his own sadism as secondary to his feeling that he had been rejected by a desired mother. The vicissitudes of his early development precluded him from making use of an approach that aimed at helping him lift repression.

Most of Winnicott's major theoretical contributions were concerned with how an infant's healthy development is enhanced or impeded by various types of maternal care. He suggested that the devoted mother both meets the infant's dependent needs at the appropriate times and encourages his independent strivings. By contrast, the unreliable and unavailable mother does not respond to her infant's basic needs and may try to impose her values and attitudes on the individuating child. Winnicott has clearly described the detrimental effects on a child of being raised by an unavailable mother: "At this early stage the infant does not register what is good or adaptive, but reacts to, and therefore knows about and registers, every failure of reliability. Reacting to unreliability in the infant-care process constitutes a trauma, each reaction being an interruption of the infant's 'going-on-being' and a rupture of the infant's self."[4] Elsewhere Winnicott describes the harmful consequences that ensue when a mother fails to enhance her child's need to separate from her: "The mother who is not good enough is not able to implement the infant's omnipotence, and so she repeatedly fails to meet the infant's gesture; instead she substitutes her own gesture which is to be given sense by the compliance of the infant. This compliance on the part of the infant is the earliest stage of the False Self, and belongs to the mother's inability to sense her infant's needs."[5] These two aspects of mothering—meeting the child's dependent needs and enhancing his independent development—are widely accepted, although they are often described in terms other than those used by Winnicott. Leo Stone, for example, writes of "the mother of bodily contact" and "the mother of separation."[6]

A mother who is generally unavailable and does not enhance her child's independence during the earliest stages of development does not know how to hold a useful dialogue with him during his oedipal period. In the pre-oedipal period the child discovers that he cannot count on this type of mother to mitigate his tension or encourage his strivings to become autonomous. Such a mother is not capable of helping him cope with

4. Donald Winnicott (1963), Morals and Education, in Winnicott (1965), *The Maturation Process and Facilitative Environment*, New York: International Universities Press, p. 97.

5. Donald Winnicott (1950), Ego Distortion or the True and False Self, in Winnicott (1965), p. 145.

6. Leo Stone (1961), *The Psychoanalytic Situation*, New York: International Universities Press.

the feelings of desire and anger evoked during the oedipal period. A mother who "does not meet the infant's gesture" does not help him acquire meaningful ways of expressing the less archaic aspects of his instinctual wishes.

Guntrip was a highly creative and generally well functioning individual, not a severely disturbed person. Someone must have been responsive to some aspects of his basic needs during his development. He states that his father was supportive and that his mother never lost her temper in his presence. Nonetheless, the almost total absence of helpful interchanges with his mother during the pre-oedipal and oedipal periods apparently kept him from using repression as a major mode of defense. Because he had not been helped to deploy the selective and sophisticated mechanism of repression in his childhood, he was incapable of appreciating what an analyst was asking him to accomplish in lifting repression.

Winnicott himself believed that the failure of Guntrip's mother to respond to his early needs influenced his development and shaped his character, particularly his excessive and compulsive need to be active. Winnicott acted as if he believed that Guntrip's oedipal issues and conflicts were less consequential and less pertinent to his development than these early issues. He did not persist in trying to interpret Guntrip's sadism, ruthlessness, and aggression as aspects of his instinctual wishes.

A comparison of Freud's famous case of the Rat Man (1909) with that of Guntrip highlights the importance of relatively healthy dialogues in childhood for deploying repression and for lifting it in the analytic situation. We have only limited information about the Rat Man's interactions, let alone his dialogues, with the significant people who brought him up. He did, however, report to Freud:

> When I was six years old I already suffered from erections, and I know that once I went to my mother to complain

> about them. I know too that in doing so I had some misgivings to get over, for I had a feeling that there was some connection between this subject and my ideas and inquisitiveness, and at the time I used to have a morbid idea *that my parents knew my thoughts; I explained this to myself by supposing that I had spoken them out loud, without having heard myself do it.* (pp. 161–162)

There are complex reasons why a boy would "complain" to his mother about having erections. The Rat Man may have been trying to evoke his mother's sexual interest in him or at least find out whether she would react favorably to the idea that his penis had become erect. Nonetheless, his stated concern about his parents' knowing his thoughts indicates that he was also concerned about their reactions to his sexual feelings. He may have told his mother about his erections to ascertain whether she would be critical of his sexuality or even whether she would help him understand why he had them and why he had a "very strong *wish to see [girls] naked*" (p. 162). We do not know how his mother responded to his complaint, but the fact that he felt free enough to tell her about his erections suggests that she was considerably more accessible to him than Guntrip's mother was to Guntrip.

Freud's case report indicates that there were favorable aspects to the Rat Man's relationship with his father. This inference is supported by the fact that the Rat Man readily established a useful therapeutic relationship with Freud. Even though the relationship with his father did not result in his developing a solid, self-confident identity, he apparently could turn to his father when he was upset for help in making sense out of what he was experiencing. In a previous discussion of this case I stated:

> His compulsive rituals had all the features of a man carrying on a frantic dialogue with himself. This inner dialogue,

> conducted now with himself, was undoubtedly at one time, in one form or another, carried on with his father. The original aim of this dialogue was on the part of the father to help the boy control his rage and passivity, and on the part of the boy to find a way to avoid the disastrous state of affairs created by his fantasies and impulsive actions.[7]

This dialogue did not result in his acquiring in adult life helpful and meaningful ways to express his sexuality and aggression. Nonetheless, the fact that he internalized aspects of his dialogues with his father suggests that his interactions with him were valuable. Moreover, these interactions served as the basis for establishing the kind of a dialogue with Freud that resulted in his lifting repression of his sexuality and sadism.

Whereas the Rat Man's pre-oedipal period was less traumatic than Guntrip's and his family more intact, his oedipal period was marred by the death of a favorite older sister. It is quite likely that her death, and his family's reaction to it, intensified his sexual and aggressive conflicts. At that time his parents would have been preoccupied and upset, and they would not have been able to relate to him in helpful ways. In all probability he was experiencing intense and conflicted wishes and feelings, including sadistic ones, in reaction to these events. The relative absence of his parents would have increased his sense of helplessness, and he could not turn to them for help in expressing the less primitive aspects of his sexuality and aggression. His helplessness and anxiety would have made it necessary for him to try to keep the archaic aspects of his instincts "at a distance from the conscious." The Rat Man himself noted that his behavior changed around this period of his life, and he avoided situations that evoked intense desire and anger. When it was no

7. Paul G. Myerson (1966), Comment on Dr. Zetzel's Paper, *Int. J. Psycho-Analysis* 47, pp. 134–142.

longer possible to keep from experiencing his libidinal and aggressive wishes, he became symptomatic.

What is striking about the Rat Man is the ease with which he established a working alliance with Freud and the rapidity with which he became aware of and tolerated his own sadism. Moreover, unlike many other analysands, he quickly accepted responsibility for what he was experiencing, though not all at once. It is worthwhile again to examine what transpired in this analysis and to evaluate what each of the two participants contributed to its favorable outcome.

Early in the analysis Freud told the Rat Man that his sense of guilt "belongs to some other content, which is unknown and which requires to be looked for" (1909, p. 176). Freud was suggesting that the Rat Man's preoccupation with his failure to return Lieutenant A's eyeglasses concealed a threatening and conflicted wish. He reports the Rat Man's reply:

> When he was twelve years old he had been in love with a little girl, the sister of a friend of his. (In answer to a question he said that his love had not been sensual; he had not wanted to see her naked, because she was too small.) But she had not shown him as much affection as he desired. And thereupon the idea had come to him that she would be kind to him if some misfortune were to befall him; and as an instance of such a misfortune his father's death had forced itself upon his mind. He had at once rejected the idea with energy. And even now he could not admit the possibility that what had arisen in this way could have been a "wish"; it had been clearly no more than a "train of thought." (p. 178)

The Rat Man's "idea" had permitted him to hold on to his desire that this girl would be "kind" to him. It allowed him to remain in the situation that evoked conflicted wishes he had by no means resolved during his oedipal period. The girl's lack of affection for him had revived the anger he had both toward his mother for not having reciprocated his desire and toward his father for having won out over him. At the time he told Freud this incident, he was unaware of these sources of his anger. He saw his "train of thought," which led to the "misfortune" of his father's death, as aimed at eliciting the girl's sympathy. Clearly, he still did not accept responsibility either for a "wish" that culminated in his father's death or for the sadism he directed toward the girl. Moreover, he reported that the idea of his father's death had "forced itself upon his mind" and that "he had at once rejected [it] . . . with energy." Nonetheless, the fantasy is indicative of his active efforts to cope with his intense feelings of desire and anger. The compromise he had arrived at would not be useful for establishing an intimate heterosexual relationship, yet he was actively striving to structure and make sense out of what he was experiencing.

Freud told the Rat Man that his guilt was related to an unknown wish. It is my belief that at this stage of the analytic dialogue the analysand was not ready to acknowledge the nature of this wish. Yet he responded to Freud by recalling that he once had an idea about his father's dying. His recollection of the idea, even though he could not admit it was a wish, indicates that he had already come to view Freud as someone who could help him sort out his feelings.

In contrast with Winnicott (in his analysis of Guntrip), Freud emphasized the importance of his analysand's becoming aware of his "primitive sadism." He had a theory about the genesis of neurotic symptoms and had developed a technique for alleviating them. The analysis of the Rat Man was for Freud, and for most analysts, a vivid illustration of his theory and his technique. Freud was quite direct in letting the Rat Man know what he expected him to accomplish in his analysis. He told the Rat Man that the edicts and prohibitions with which he was obsessed represented a concealed and unconscious wish. The

Rat Man's preoccupations, Freud said, showed that he was behaving much like the police, who "when they cannot catch the right murderer, arrest a wrong one instead" (p. 176). He categorically stated that if the Rat Man was to recover from his illness, he would have to catch the right murderer by paying attention to the wish he had repressed.

Once the Rat Man realized what type of analytic work Freud was expecting him to accomplish, he voiced his concern that discovering the concealed wish would only cause him distress. Freud took this concern quite seriously. He went into lengthy explanations about the genesis of the Rat Man's illness and indicated why recognition of its origins would be of great value to him.

After making the analogy between doing analysis and catching the right murderer, Freud stated:

> [The Rat Man] brought forth a few doubts.—How, he asked, could the information that the self-reproach, the sense of guilt, was justified have a therapeutic effect?—I explained that it was not the information that had this effect, but the discovery of the unknown content to which the self-reproach was really attached.—Yes, he said, that was the precise point to which his question had been directed.—I then made some short observations on the *psychological differences between the conscious and the unconscious,* and upon the fact that everything conscious is subject to the process called wearing away, while what was unconscious was relatively unchangeable; and I illustrated my remarks by pointing to the antiques standing about in my room. They were, in fact, I said, only objects found in a tomb, and their burial had been their preservation: the destruction of Pompeii was only beginning now that it had been dug up. (p. 176)

In the same charming if somewhat didactic vein, Freud was trying to convince the Rat Man that in becoming aware of the wish concealed by his self-reproach, he would diminish rather than increase his distress.

Having suggested to the Rat Man that his idea about his father's death represented a wish rather than a "train of thought," he explains that the Rat Man

> was quite certain that his father's death could never have been an object of his desire but only of his fear.—After his forcible enunciation of these words, I thought it advisable to bring a fresh piece of theory to his notice. According to psycho-analytic theory, I told him, every fear corresponds to a former wish which is now repressed; we are therefore obliged to believe the exact contrary of what he had asserted. This would fit in with another theoretical requirement, namely, that the unconscious must be the precise contrary of the conscious. He was much agitated at this and very incredulous. He wondered how he could possibly have had such a wish, considering that he loved his father more than anyone else in the world; there could be no doubt that he would have renounced all his own prospects of happiness if by so doing he could have saved his father's life.—I answered that it was precisely such intense love as his that was a necessary condition of his hatred. (pp. 179–180)

Freud did more than offer the Rat Man a "fresh piece of theory." He attempted to mitigate the Rat Man's concern that if he were to experience and acknowledge his hatred for his father, he would see his relationship with his father as negative. Freud told him that he loved his father as well as hated him. He stated that he himself was aware of the Rat Man's love for his father and of his capacity to love in general. In making these statements during the early phases of the analysis, Freud indicated that he could help the Rat Man understand and "wear away" the feelings and fantasies threatening him. Freud conveyed his confidence in his analysand's ability to make use of an approach aimed at lifting repression and, in addition, his appreciation of the Rat Man's fundamental decency. Here Freud was directly addressing his analysand's concerns about becoming engaged in the analytic work of lifting repression. Even at this early stage of the analysis, these concerns were not far from the Rat Man's consciousness. He recognized what Freud expected of him, but he was reluctant to direct his attention to a wish to kill his father. The Rat Man's early awareness of the demands of analytic work suggests that at some point in his development he had had relatively healthy dialogues with one or another of his parents or caretakers. During at least one period of his childhood someone had been uncritical of him and had not rejected his appeals for help in coping with and understanding aspects of his sexuality and aggression.

Freud's efforts to mitigate his analysand's concerns did no more than set the stage for enacting the analytic process. Freud asserts:

> It is never the aim of discussions like this to create conviction. They are only intended to bring the repressed complexes into consciousness, to set the conflict going in the field of conscious mental activity, and to facilitate the emergence of fresh material from the unconscious. A sense of conviction is only attained after the patient has himself worked over the reclaimed material, and so long as he is not fully convinced the material must be considered as unexhausted. (p. 181 n. 1)

No matter how benevolently the analyst presents himself and how helpful he actually is, the analysand will inevitably react to him and experience him as if he were not reciprocating his desire and were critical of him for having these desires. Of course, these reactions serve as the basis of the analyst's mutative interpretations, which convince the analysand that the sexual and aggressive wishes his analyst has been pointing out to him are valid aspects of himself.

In the course of his analysis the Rat Man experienced important aspects of his repressed wishes. Freud reports:

> It was only along the painful road of transference that he was able to reach a conviction that his relationship with his father really necessitated the postulation of this unconscious complement. He even reached a point at which, in his dreams, his waking phantasies, and his associations, he began heaping the grossest and filthiest abuse upon me and my family, though in his deliberate actions he never treated me with anything but the greatest respect. Thus, little by little, in this school of suffering, the patient won the sense of conviction which he had lacked—though to any disinterested mind the truth would have been almost self-evident. (p. 209)

Any experienced analyst would agree that a "sense of conviction" can only occur in a "school of suffering." Yet the analysand will inevitably be reluctant to enroll in a school that causes him to revive and relive what is painful. Before becoming engaged in the work of lifting repression, he needs to be convinced that something besides suffering will come from this activity. But first the analyst must address the analysand's concerns about placing himself in a vulnerable position, where he is expected to experience and observe repressed and archaic aspects of desire and anger. It is essential that the analyst mitigate the analysand's fear of being left helpless with, criticized for, or considered only in the light of the wishes he is being encouraged to recognize.

If Guntrip's version of his relationship with his mother is reasonably accurate, even Freud, with all his magnetism and with his conviction in the validity of his theory, probably would not have succeeded in engaging him in the work of lifting repression. Guntrip was two and a half years old when his brother Percy was born and three and a half when he died. He was told later that he himself collapsed and almost died after Percy's death. He had a complete amnesia for these events.

Guntrip quotes Winnicott as saying to him during the second analysis, "You must have had an earlier illness before Percy was born and felt mother left you to look after yourself. You accepted Percy as your infant self that needed looking after. When he died you had nothing and collapsed." Guntrip told Winnicott that "people often commented on my ceaseless activity and energy and that in sessions I did not like gaps of silence and at times talked hard." Winnicott replied, "Your problem is that the illness of collapse was never resolved. You had to keep yourself alive in spite of it. You cannot take your ongoing being for granted. You have to work hard to keep yourself in existence. You are afraid to stop acting, talking, or keeping awake. You feel you might die in a gap like Percy because if you stop acting mother cannot do anything. She could not save Percy or you" (Guntrip 1975, p. 152).

In Winnicott's view, Guntrip had sustained himself by his "ceaseless activity" and by caring for his younger brother as he wanted to have been cared for himself. He could not turn to his mother for love, let alone for help in coping with and understanding the intense feelings evoked by her lack of ordinary care. As a result, he did not deploy repression as a primary defense.

Elsewhere I have discussed the genetic circumstances that foster a person's potential for accepting responsibility for the more archaic aspects of his desire and anger:

> To accept responsibility for a feeling of desire or anger—to account for it by acknowledging it as belonging to oneself—the child will need to have had someone else acknowledge that what he is experiencing is not solely caused by him, that it is not "all his fault." . . . Moreover, to realize that he is not totally responsible for all the consequences of his desire and anger, the child will also need to have someone encourage, approve of, at least permit him

> to express his desire and anger. He needs this type of encouragement in order for him to discover for himself that if he acts upon or expresses his desire and anger, sometimes at least, no one will hurt him or be hurt by him or reject him and that even when someone is upset by his actions, that other person will bear some responsibility for this reaction.[8]

I hypothesized that someone who has not been helped to place feelings of desire and anger in a meaningful context will not develop a sense of himself as the agent responsible for his incestuous and murderous wishes; he will repress memories of events that have happened to him. In contrast with someone with a more favorable development, he will not turn his attention away from the notion that his wishes have brought about a catastrophe—the essence of the process of using repression. If this individual is eventually able to lift repression he will recover traumatic moments; but he will not be able to recover a sense of himself as the agent of his archaic desires or feelings of aggression.

After Winnicott's death, Guntrip, through associating to his dreams, eventually recovered the memory of his brother's death and his reactions to it: "I had recovered in that dream the memory of collapsing when I saw him as a dead object and reached out to grab him. But I had done more; I had actually gone back in both dreams to the early time before he died, to see the faceless depersonalized mother, and the black depressed mother, who totally failed to relate to both of us" (Guntrip 1975, p. 154). Toward the end of his life, Guntrip became capable, in large part through his treatment with Winnicott, of lifting the repression of painful, traumatic events. He did not,

8. Paul G. Myerson (1981), The Nature of the Transactions That Occur in Other than a Classical Analysis. *Int. Rev. Psycho-Analysis* 8, p. 178.

however, recall desiring his mother or being angry at her because she had rejected his affection.

Analysts who use a classical approach would consider Guntrip's reaction to his brother in terms of sibling rivalry. They would believe that Guntrip was angry at his mother for replacing him with another child and would emphasize Guntrip's jealousy and sadistic wishes toward the sibling. They would construe Guntrip's caring attention to his brother as a means of undoing his aggression. They would postulate that because Guntrip's sadism toward his mother and brother jeopardized his relationship with his mother, he must have employed various mechanisms of defense, including repression, to maintain his relationship with her. Moreover, classical analysts would suggest that Guntrip's collapse after his brother's actual death represented his guilty reaction to his wishes toward the hated sibling.

Guntrip, and apparently Winnicott, did not share this view of Guntrip's development. Guntrip believed instead that his mother had never offered him adequate care and love during his first years. When his brother was born, he compensated for this lack of love by actively caring for his brother and by serving as his surrogate mother. Guntrip considered his mother to be unavailable. In this situation there was no sense elaborating and reporting his dreams and fantasies to ascertain whether she would help him tolerate and understand what he was experiencing. There were no helpful dialogues to be held with a mother who was remote, depressed, and unempathic. He relinquished this possibility and altered his behavior and the ways in which he related to others. He compensated for his mother's absence by ceaseless activity and by caring for other people.

Practicing psychoanalysts soon realize that many of those who consult them do not have typically neurotic personality structures. Winnicott (1965), Fairbairn, Kohut, and Guntrip himself have described some of these vicissitudes of development.[9] They all address issues relevant to persons whose parents have failed them in significant ways. They are concerned with those who lacked the opportunity to have the kind of a dialogue with a helpful parent that would have enhanced their potential to accept responsibility for their instinctual wishes and to deploy and lift the repression of these wishes. This failure made it necessary for them to use more global and primitive measures of defense, which greatly influence the way they behave and relate to others. Under these circumstances, a psychoanalytic approach aimed at lifting repression is of limited value at best.

The classical approach, where analysts interpret with the aim of helping analysands lift repression of their instinctual wishes and where they encourage analysands to experience and observe their repressed desire and anger, is effective in helping neurotic individuals make meaningful changes. Most personalities, however, cannot be reduced to a contrast between neurosis and developmental deficit. In later chapters I will attempt to demonstrate that there are many individuals whose best interests are served when their analysts shift from the classical approach to another or, in some instances, employ a combination of approaches.

9. W. R. D. Fairbairn (1954), *An Object-Relations Theory of Personality*, New York: Basic Books; Heinz Kohut (1971), *The Analysis of the Self*, New York: International Universities Press; Harry Guntrip (1961), *Schizoid Phenomena, Object Relations, and the Self*, New York: International Universities Press.

2 The Analyst's Contribution to the Lifting of Repression

In the previous chapter I emphasized those interactions in which the analyst interprets in order to help the analysand actively direct his attention to the ways in which he experiences his repressed wishes. On such occasions it is the analyst's intention to increase the analysand's willingness to experience and then to observe the affective components of his sexual desire and anger that are emerging from repression. Since insight is most effective therapeutically when it is an affective process, it is important that the analyst encourage the analysand to experience the feelings associated with his repressed wishes and to recognize the context in which they occur. It is only through this process that the analysand comes to acquire a meaningful understanding of himself.

As I have already noted, Freud pointed out that the analytic situation itself "facilitate[s] the emergence of fresh material from the unconscious." The analytic rule that the analysand say everything that comes to mind and that the analyst refrain from directly gratifying the wishes expressed in the analysand's associations evokes reactions similar to those the analysand experienced as a child toward those people who frustrated his desire for them. These analytic conditions promote aspects of the analysand's repressed wishes. Yet it is necessary for him to pay active attention to these wishes and to tolerate as well as experience them. The analyst enhances this second step of the process of lifting repression through his interpretive activity, especially his efforts to encourage and persuade the analysand to observe what he is experiencing.

The views set forth in this chapter are rooted in the assumptions that the analysand has the capacity to observe his own mental processes and that the analyst, for his part, is relatively clear about his intention in making interpretations. (Later I will discuss other situations in which these assumptions are not valid.) Even where these two favorable conditions are present, they are not sufficient in themselves for the analysand to become engaged in the process of lifting repression. He must first be provided with a frame of reference or context that will allow him to make sense out of what he is experiencing. The analyst may offer a clarification to help him recognize a connection between an antecedent external event and his subsequent reactions to it. For example, the analyst may suggest to the analysand that his coming late to a session is related to the fact that on the preceding day the analyst had announced his forthcoming vacation. The analyst's immediate purpose in highlighting this link is to enhance the analysand's realization that his behavior is motivated, that there is a reason for his late arrival. It is clear that the analyst is hoping to promote the analysand's ability to test reality so that he will be better able to discriminate between the actual analytic situation, where he is being given an explanation for his coming late, and a fantasized situation in which he fears he will be criticized for that behavior.

The analysand's recognition that these links exist is essential for his subsequent willingness to experience and pay attention to the affective components of his own repressed wishes. His recognition that his reactions have causes and that he can evaluate their consequences offers him a context for his behavior. This context provides the sense of security he needs in order to experience the emerging affective elements of his desire and anger (Myerson 1981).

After the analyst has promoted the analysand's recognition of this context, he will encourage him to allow himself to experience the affective elements of his instinctual wishes. He may suggest to the analysand that his late arrival for the appointment indicates that he is feeling angrier at the analyst than he had realized. The analysand may respond to this interpretation by recalling that he had actually felt angry at the analyst while driving away from the previous session, in which he had been told about the analyst's forthcoming vacation. He may further recall that he had been tempted to suppress this feeling of anger because he was concerned that acknowledging it to the analyst would impair their relationship. In this case the analysand is obviously demonstrating a degree of willingness to do the analytic work involved in paying attention to the ways he experiences his repressed anger.

But an analysand may be unwilling to become involved in analytic work after being offered an interpretation of this kind. When the analysand clearly understands what is expected of him and yet is unwilling to engage in the analytic work, he may be concerned that the analyst will not be willing or able to help him tolerate his repressed feelings. He may fear that he will become helpless to cope with the intense feelings of desire and anger that he has allowed himself to experience. This concern may be compounded by his uncertainty as to whether the analyst will respond to his acknowledgment of these feelings in a critical or rejecting manner. He may also be uncertain about whether the analyst will recognize that he has strengths in addition to feelings about which he is conflicted. In particular, he may be concerned that the analyst will not appreciate that he is making an effort to cooperate in the work of lifting repression. In these situations the analysand may be dubious about the analyst's availability to help him tolerate his repressed desire or anger. Yet even where the analysand does not anticipate rejection, criticism, or lack of appreciation from the analyst, he may remain fearful of being abandoned with the feelings and fantasies he has repressed up to this point.

I am focusing on those analytic transactions in which the analysand realizes that he is expected to pay attention to the way he experiences his repressed wishes and then communicates to the analyst his reluctance to do so. In such transactions the analysand indicates his concerns in an attempt to ascertain whether the analyst is able and willing to address them. The analysand may express his concerns directly: he may state that he does not see any value in becoming more aware of his anger or that he is not convinced that the analyst could retain a therapeutic attitude if he were to acknowledge his angry feelings toward him. More typically, however, the analysand may indicate his concerns indirectly, perhaps in the form of displacement. For example, he may talk about a friend who did not receive a promotion after he had expressed resentment toward a superior at work.

The crucial element in these transactions is whether the analyst becomes aware of and addresses the analysand's concerns. If the analyst is aware of these concerns, he may clarify their nature and encourage the analysand to examine their validity. The analyst's act of clarification may indicate that he will remain helpful and not leave the analysand unsupported in the face of the feelings he has allowed himself to experience. Under these conditions the alliance becomes stronger and the analysand more willing to put himself in the vulnerable position of paying attention to the ways in which he experiences his repressed wishes. But if the analyst is not aware that the analysand is demonstrating his concerns about placing himself in this vulnerable position, he loses the opportunity to address them. The analysand then becomes increasingly reluctant to pay attention to the analytic work, leaving the analyst and analysand to function at cross-purposes rather than develop a meaningful alliance.

The differences in the ways Freud applied his approach in the cases of Dora[1] in 1905 and the Rat Man in 1909 illustrate his growing sense that it was necessary to address the analysand's concerns about lifting repression. In his treatment of Dora, Freud insisted that his analysand pay attention to various manifestations of her repressed desires without clarifying the purpose of her doing so and without addressing her concerns about it. His insistence that she overcome her resistance created an atmosphere in which she was unwilling to do the analytic work of lifting her repression.

Freud states that it is the unobjectionable component of the analysand's positive transference that is the basis for his willingness to do the analytic work. Merton Gill makes the same point except that he labels it the "facilitating transference."[2] They both distinguish this type of transference from the erotic and negative transferences that underlie the various types of resistance analysands manifest in regard to doing the analytic work. Freud noted that analysands develop an unobjectionable positive transference with relative ease provided that the analyst remains nonjudgmental and neither sides with nor criticizes the analysand. I would like to make the point, however, that the analyst's lack of awareness of his analysand's concerns about becoming involved in the analytic work, especially in situations where he insists that the analysand overcome his resistance, seriously interferes with the analysand's developing the kind of transference associated with a willingness to lift repression.

By the time Freud treated the Rat Man, he was very much

1. Sigmund Freud (1905), Fragment of an Analysis of a Case of Hysteria, S.E. 7, pp. 7–122.

2. Merton Gill (1982), *Analysis of Transference,* New York: International Universities Press.

aware that it was necessary to address an analysand's concerns. As I observed in chapter 1, Freud made quite clear to the Rat Man what he thought had caused his symptomatology and what the analysand needed to do to recover from his illness. He also demonstrated a warm and human interest in the analysand's welfare. Moreover, he encouraged the Rat Man to play an active part in the process of lifting his repression. But we must acknowledge that Freud sometimes actively persuaded his analysand to experience and understand the libidinal and aggressive wishes that he had precluded from his awareness. Freud appeared at times to insist that the Rat Man become involved in the analytic work. He told the Rat Man that he was reluctant to entertain the idea that he wished his father to die; in fact, the Rat Man indicated to Freud that if he were to have such thoughts, they would be the death of him. Freud replied that he "must never lose sight of the fact that a treatment like ours proceeded to the accompaniment of a *constant resistance*" (1909, p. 184). Freud emphasized that he should be repeatedly reminding the Rat Man of this fact. Yet Freud also repeatedly demonstrated his willingness to clarify the Rat Man's concerns about lifting his repression and address them in a helpful way. We can, I believe, consider Freud's overall attitude to be more encouraging than insistent.

I consider that the most meaningful changes within a psychoanalysis occur when the analyst has successfully encouraged the analysand to tolerate and accept responsibility for the desire and anger he had previously shut out of his awareness. This change involves a profound alteration in the analysand's state of mind. It is likely to occur when the analyst has succeeded in encouraging the analysand's active participation in the analytic work by addressing and mitigating his concerns about becoming involved in it.

James Strachey, in his groundbreaking paper "The Nature of the Therapeutic Action of Psychoanalysis" ([1934] 1969), emphasizes other elements of the analytic process than I do. In Strachey's formulation, the analyst does not appear to encourage the analysand to play an active role in lifting his repression. The analysand is in a relatively passive position, especially during the first part of the process. Strachey states that the analyst "gives permission for a small quantity of id-energy (in our instance, in the form of an aggressive impulse) to become conscious." Strachey at another point notes, "In the classical model of an interpretation, the patient will first be made aware of a state of tension in his ego, will next be made aware that there is a repressive factor at work (that his superego is threatening him with punishment), and will only then be made aware of the id-impulse which has stirred up the protests of his superego and so given rise to the anxiety in his ego" (p. 283).

I believe that when an analyst encourages the analysand to pay attention to the way he experiences his repressed wishes, he is involving the analysand in a process quite different from when the analyst gives permission to him to express an impulse or makes him aware of his unconscious conflicts. In the latter instances, the analyst promotes a situation in which the analysand plays an essentially passive role. Strachey does not depict the analyst and analysand as engaging in a dialogue about the feasibility and value of the analysand's lifting his repression. Moreover, he does not consider the analyst's role to be one of listening for and then addressing the analysand's concerns about becoming aware of the nature of his unconscious conflicts. In Strachey's formulation, the analyst permits the analysand to become conscious of his "id-energy" but does not encourage him to participate in the process. If the analyst does not listen to the analysand's concerns and does not evaluate the extent of the analysand's willingness to participate, he is likely to insist that the analysand lift his repression rather than encourage him to do so.

Furthermore, if the analyst acts in accord with Strachey's

formulation, he is likely to judge the success of his interpretive endeavor in terms of whether the analysand has acknowledged his awareness of the particular aspect of his desire and anger that was the subject of the interpretation. The analyst who holds this perspective does not consider the quality of the analysand's awareness; he does not take into account how adequately the analysand accepts and assumes responsibility for what he has become aware of or how capable he is of tolerating, rather than immediately resolving, what he has recognized in himself. I believe this is particularly true when the analyst urges the analysand to test the appropriateness of that aspect of his desire and anger of which he has become aware. In fact, Strachey states that after the analysand has become conscious of his impulse toward the analyst, he immediately engages in reality-testing: "If all goes well, the patient's ego will become aware of the contrast between the aggressive character of his feelings and the real nature of the analyst who does not behave like the patient's 'good' or 'bad' archaic object. The patient, that is to say, will become aware of a distinction between his archaic phantasy object and the real external object" (p. 283).

Strachey maintains that once the analysand has been given permission to express his anger, he will realize that the analyst's actual behavior does not warrant the degree of anger he has felt toward him. The analysand will be able to discriminate between the analyst's actual actions and those he has attributed to his "archaic phantasy object." Strachey assigns a crucial curative role to reality-testing. He states that the patient who has "become aware of the lack of aggressiveness in the real external object will be able to diminish his own aggressiveness; the new object which he introjects will be less aggressive, and consequently the aggressiveness of the superego will also be diminished" (p. 283).

Strachey's formulation implies that once the analysand has been given permission to express his anger, he will test the reality of the analytic situation in a way that actually diminishes his anger toward the analyst. He will become less angry at the analyst because he will realize that the analyst had not intended to harm him when, let us say, he informed the analysand of his vacation plans as well as that the analyst is not going to be critical of him when the analysand acknowledges his angry reaction.

Strachey is describing the effects of reality-testing in the light of a Kleinian orientation, particularly when he writes about the analysand's introjecting a new, less aggressive object as a means of diminishing his own aggressiveness. For our purposes, however, the essential point of Strachey's formulation is that the analysand focuses his attention on the analyst's behavior and in so doing differentiates the way the analyst actually behaves from the behavior he had anticipated. According to Strachey, the analysand pays attention to the characteristics of an external object and not to how he himself experiences his repressed wishes toward that object.

There is, of course, no reason an analysand cannot focus his attention in more than one direction. The process I have highlighted does not exclude the one Strachey has delineated. I do not wish to minimize the significance of reality-testing, which may be very useful in and of itself. Moreover, as I have suggested earlier, the analysand's newly developed ability to link an internal event with antecedent and subsequent external events may give him the sense of security necessary to be able to experience his repressed wishes. Yet there are important differences between these two ways of formulating what takes place when an analyst offers an interpretation to an analysand. One of these is due to differing metapsychologies. Strachey's analyst gives permission for a small quantity of the analysand's id-energy to become conscious. The analyst I envision encourages the analysand to pay attention to what he is experiencing.

I believe that this metapsychological issue can be reconciled without great difficulty. There is a more fundamental difference, however, between these two formulations of the nature of the analytic process. In Strachey's, the analysand diminishes his aggressiveness by expressing it and therefore is able to realize that the actions of the external object—the analyst—do not warrant his feeling so angry. I believe this represents a different process from one where the analysand is helped to tolerate and accept responsibility for his repressed wishes. In my formulation, the analyst encourages the analysand to pay attention to the ways in which he experiences these wishes. As I have indicated, the analysand will be concerned about being placed in a vulnerable position. When the analyst mitigates these concerns, the analysand will become more willing not only to pay attention to what he has experienced but also to tolerate and accept responsibility for his repressed wishes. Under these conditions, the analysand does not so much diminish his aggressiveness as experience it in a new and more meaningful state of mind. He tolerates the aggressiveness he has allowed himself to experience, realizing that it is a part of himself that does not disappear just because he can recognize that certain aspects of it are at times exaggerated reactions to real events.

An analyst who functions in accord with Strachey's formulation may place pressure on the analysand to diminish the intensity of his wishes before the analysand has had the opportunity to pay attention to their more repressed aspects. It is true that the analysand may realize once he has expressed his anger at the analyst that the analyst will not in fact criticize him or reject him for having done so. According to Strachey, however, this analysand is also expected to realize that his anger at the analyst is unwarranted—for example, that it would be inappropriate for him, after being told that the analyst is going on a vacation, to wish that the analyst's plane would crash. In those instances when the analyst implies to the analysand that his anger is inappropriate, it is likely that the analysand will feel that the analyst is being critical of him. Under these circumstances, the analysand is unlikely to be willing to attempt to deepen his awareness or to experience the still-repressed aspects of his desire and anger.

Strachey, it should be recalled, seeks to trace the fate of an "aggressive impulse that reaches consciousness." He states, "With a view to clarity of exposition, I shall take as an instance the interpretation of a hostile impulse. By virtue of his power (his strictly limited power) as auxiliary superego, the analyst gives permission for a certain small quantity of the patient's id-energy (in our instance in the form of an aggressive impulse) to become conscious" (p. 283). Strachey might have modified his formulation if he had traced the fate of libidinal impulses under similar circumstances. I believe there is a difference between becoming aware of one's intense anger toward the analyst in response to hearing about his vacation and becoming aware of a desire to go on the vacation with the analyst.

The relationship between desire and anger is complex. I am by no means suggesting that anger is manifest only when a desire of one type or another is frustrated or unreciprocated. That would downplay the importance of envy and competitive strivings. The analysand in fact is in a far more vulnerable position when he is being encouraged to experience his desire for the analyst than when he is being encouraged to experience his anger toward him. In both situations the analysand will be concerned about the possibility of being abandoned and about becoming overwhelmed by the feelings he is being encouraged to experience. Yet the analyst can more readily address and mitigate the analysand's concerns about experiencing his anger. The analysand's reality is notably different in the two situations. By and large, the analyst will be helpful and will not be critical of him if the analysand allows himself to experience his anger toward him and can acknowledge it. The analyst, sooner or later, will clarify the analysand's concerns about experiencing his anger in a way that shows his nonjudgmental, nonrejecting, and helpful attitude. The analyst's attitude will help the analysand realize that he is not being abandoned even though he is experiencing angry feelings toward the analyst.

The analysand will have a different perception of the analyst's attitude, however, when he has allowed himself to experience desire for the analyst. Although the analyst in this situation is nonjudgmental and accepting of the fact that the analysand feels desire for him, it is unavoidable that the analysand will feel to some extent abandoned and left to cope by himself with his feelings of desire for the analyst. The analysand cannot, in Strachey's terms, "introject" the nondesiring analyst in a manner that diminishes his own desire. It is therefore not remarkable that an analysand whose analyst is encouraging him to lift the repression of his desire for him might experience the analyst as attempting to put him into a situation in which he will feel humiliated and abandoned.

Under these circumstances, the analysand is more likely to pay attention to the anger he feels toward the analyst than to his desire for him. He is apt to try to diminish his anger through reality-testing. This attempt may be of value to him, but unfortunately it allows him to avoid recognizing the connection between his anger and his still-unconscious desire for the analyst. The analyst himself may be reluctant to encourage the analysand to pay attention to this desire. He himself may feel extremely vulnerable after finding himself the object of a desire that he is unable to reciprocate. The analyst's vulnerability is likely to lead him to encourage the analysand to pay attention to his anger in a way that allows him to diminish its intensity but avoid realizing the relationship of this anger to his unrequited desire for the analyst.

If an analysand is to develop a fruitful transference neurosis, one that recapitulates the conflicts that occurred during his oedipal period, it is essential for him to experience his unrequited desire for the analyst and to tolerate it. He must recognize that a significant aspect of his anger at the analyst is related to the fact that the analyst is not reciprocating his desire for him. Yet it is often very difficult for the analyst to promote the analysand's willingness to experience and pay attention to his desire. Strachey's approach, with its emphasis on the therapeutic benefits of diminishing anger, runs the risk of limiting the analysand's willingness to experience his repressed desire.

Merton Gill, in *Analysis of Transference* (1982), advocates an approach that is similar in many ways to Strachey's. Gill is interested in the transactional aspects of the analytic process. He discusses those analytic interactions in which the analyst helps the analysand overcome his resistance to doing the analytic work. He highlights two types of resistance that he maintains the analysand will inevitably manifest in the course of an analysis—first the analysand's resistance to becoming aware of the transference and then his resistance to resolving the transference.

Gill reminds us that the analytic situation itself promotes the inherent tendency of the analysand to manifest transference reactions. He emphasizes the direct impact of the analyst's actions, or lack of them, on the analysand. According to Gill, the analysand's desire and anger will inevitably be evoked by what the analyst does or does not do. He contends that the analysand will resist becoming aware of his desire and anger because of his "difficulty in recognizing erotic and hostile impulses toward the very person to whom they have to be disclosed" (p. 59). Gill then goes on to argue that the analyst himself will resist becoming aware of his analysand's transference because "the patient is likely to attribute to him the very attitudes that are most likely to cause him discomfort" (p. 59). He concludes: "The resistance to the awareness of these attitudes is responsible for their appearing in various disguises in the patient's manifest associations and for the analyst's reluctance to unmask these disguises" (p. 60). These disguises, which Gill refers to as "allusion[s] to the transference," occur when the analysand has displaced his strong emotional reactions toward the analyst onto someone else.

The nature of the analytic situation, and especially the actions or lack of actions of the analyst, evokes erotic and hostile transferences in the analysand. These reactions are manifested in a disguised form rather than directly expressed because both parties in the transaction are anxious about talking about the "erotic and hostile impulses" the analysand has toward the analyst. Gill maintains that the analyst should overcome his own anxiety and point out to the analysand that his reactions, which he had manifested in a disguised fashion, mean or represent similar reactions he has toward the analyst.

In his book Gill offers an example of what he terms "an allusion to the transference": "A man associates about an angry outburst against his wife. The latent meaning for the analytic situation may be that he is angry about something the analyst had said but is unable to say so directly. An interpretation to that effect does not mean that the 'real' meaning of his talking about the angry outburst against his wife is that he is angry at the analyst" (pp. 64–65). Gill argues, however, that the interpretation "does mean that [the analysand] has a resistance to expressing his anger openly toward the analyst, and that the matter of his outburst against his wife appears now in his associations as a disguised way of alluding to his anger at the analyst" (p. 66). He suggests that the chief aim of the analyst's interpretation is to "unmask these disguises." He believes that "the patient has to learn that the crucial technique of analysis is to find just this latent meaning" (p. 66).

I believe there is a significant difference between an interpretation that has as its major goal helping an analysand find the latent meaning of a disguised reaction and one that has the intention of encouraging the analysand to experience the feelings that underlie or are associated with these reactions. The relationship between ascertaining a meaning for a reaction and allowing oneself to experience its affective components is complex. As I have pointed out, it is necessary for the analysand to determine a context for a reaction if he is to be secure enough to tolerate the feelings associated with it. This context will allow the analysand to make sense of his reaction. Yet the analysand, as I have also indicated, may prematurely assign a meaning to his reactions in order not to experience the more threatening and conflicted aspects of his feelings.

Gill, like Strachey, is interested in resolving the transference once the analysand has become aware of the latent meaning of his allusion. He asserts that the analyst does this by interpreting the transference as representing "a plausible explanation of something that has actually taken place between the patient and the analyst—the reality cues that are the patient's point of departure for his transference elaboration" (p. 115). Gill maintains that when the analyst interprets in this manner, he looks for cues in his interactions with the analysand that suggest to him what he has done that has evoked the analysand's disguised transference reaction. The analysand may be angry at the analyst because of something the analyst said to him or because of the way he said it. The analyst who follows Gill's approach will explain the latent meaning of the analysand's angry outburst at his wife in two ways. He first will indicate to the analysand that his outburst at his wife alludes to the fact, or means, that he is angry at the analyst. He will then point out that the analysand's anger at the analyst is a response to an earlier event, to something the analyst had said to him in the previous session.

Gill allows and even encourages the analysand to decide whether his anger at the analyst is warranted. The analysand may decide that he is justified in being angry at the analyst. Gill, unlike Strachey, does not necessarily anticipate that the analysand will be able to diminish his anger by introjecting the less aggressive aspects of the analyst once he has been given permission to express his anger and has realized that it is unwarranted. But in Gill's approach the analyst runs the risk of asking the analysand to account for his anger in a way that could seriously limit his understanding of it. In this situation the analysand's way of accounting for his anger is likely to be at the cost of recognizing and experiencing the more archaic and repressed aspects of his desire and anger.

The view Gill is advocating is prototypical of what happens in many analyses. This approach may help the analysand recognize more realistic causal links between one event and another, and this in turn may afford him the security necessary to experience the repressed aspects of his desire and anger. Yet there are circumstances where a recognition of certain causal links between one event and another could limit his willingness to experience and tolerate the more threatening aspects of his archaic wishes.

An analysand may come to the realization that he is angry at his analyst because of the tactless manner in which the analyst had earlier offered an interpretation. He may decide that his anger at the analyst is justified and may gather up his courage to tell the analyst why he is angry at him. He may then further recognize that the analyst has not become alienated by his expression of anger. In the process the analysand has been engaged in a significant type of reality-testing and has acquired an understanding of his previously disguised reaction that links it with antecedent and subsequent events. This new understanding may help the analysand cope more adequately in situations where he had previously felt disparaged and had adapted by reacting compliantly. But the analysand may also use this understanding of events to avoid experiencing important aspects of his repressed anger toward the analyst. He may not recognize that an important source of his anger at the analyst is the analyst's not reciprocating the desire the analysand has for him. In this situation the analysand is using his new understanding, which he attributes to his disguised reaction, in order not to recognize or experience his desire for the analyst or the rage he feels toward him for not reciprocating it.

Lawrence Friedman has examined Gill's concept of allusion to the transference at some length and has highlighted the nature of the analysand's mental activity that precedes the appearance of allusions in his associations.[3] Friedman points out that there is a spectrum of allusions representing the wide range of mental activities that goes on before the analysand manifests an allusion in his associations: "At one end of the spectrum are explicit, conscious, withheld thoughts, while at the other end are implications that neither party will ever be aware of—occult ways in which the patient's behavior is affected by the analyst's presence, his actions, his character, his significance, and his meaning to the patient." Friedman discusses extensively the characteristics of the mental activity that precedes an explicit allusion:

> At the explicit end of the spectrum are those occasions where the patient actively challenges his own solution to a problem. At these times the patient has in mind a specific complaint, or perhaps a plea: something addressed to the analyst to make him do one thing or avoid another; some attempt to readjust the analyst's place in the world of the patient's desire. Having addressed the analyst this way in his mind the patient nevertheless proceeds pretty much as he has already been doing. After imagining a different way of dealing with the problem, he continues to deal with it as before. In effect he has challenged his own solution but

3. Lawrence Friedman (1984), Pictures of Treatment by Gill and Schafer, *Psychoanalytic Quarterly* 53, pp. 167–207.

> decided not to accept the challenge, yet the imagined action is felt by the alert analyst. (p. 195)

Friedman is suggesting that there are times when an analysand may preconsciously imagine engaging in an action that involves the analyst but then decides not to act on what he has imagined doing. The associations he presents to the analyst may allude to this imagined new "solution to a problem," even though he chooses not to act on it. In the example cited by Gill, the analysand may have become angry over something the analyst had said to him that he considered to be a tactless remark. In accord with Friedman's ideas, he might have imagined the scene in which he confronted the analyst with his tactlessness. But because the analysand was uncertain of how the analyst would respond to being told he was tactless, he decided not to follow through with what he had imagined. Instead he talked about being angry at his wife. If the analyst had been sufficiently "alert," he would have recognized that the analysand had imagined confronting him but had decided not to do so.

From this perspective, the analyst's tactless remark is the event that immediately precedes and evokes the analysand's imagined but then rejected notion of confronting the analyst. It is important to note that in the instance being discussed, the aim of the analysand's imagined solution is, in Friedman's words, "to make [the analyst] do one thing or avoid another; to adjust the analyst's place in the world of the patient's desire." The analysand is imagining doing or saying something that he had not done or said before that will cause the analyst himself to behave more in accord with the analysand's needs and desire. He perhaps hopes to affect the analyst in such a way that he will stop hurting his feelings and interact with him in a more caring manner.

Friedman's ideas about the nature of the analysand's mental

activity underlying the allusions he makes while free-associating are of interest and valuable. But Friedman's discussion implies that the analysand's problem arises from his anxiety about how the analyst would respond if he were to complain about his behavior. He suggests that the analysand will find the solution to this problem through behaving in a manner that affects the analyst's actions rather than through lifting the repression of his instinctual wishes. According to Friedman, the analyst should listen for the allusions of the analysand that refer to the consequences he imagines would occur if he were to confront the analyst. Friedman, however, does not take into consideration those allusions that might refer to the concerns the analysand would have if he were encouraged to lift repression.

An analyst who follows Gill's and Friedman's approach will give the analysand permission to express his anger at him directly once he has helped the analysand become aware that he is alluding to his thoughts about acting in this manner. An analyst who attempts to give the analysand permission to confront him might tell him that his expressed anger toward his wife suggests that he was thinking about saying he was angry at the analyst but that he was afraid to tell him this because he was uncertain about how the analyst would react. The analyst, of course, is implying that he would not reject or criticize the analysand if he were to do so. Whatever the merits or liabilities of this type of intervention, it is crucial to realize that in offering it, the analyst's primary intention is to influence how the analysand behaves, not to help him become more aware of his feelings.

In the situation I have just described, the analysand has not been encouraged to experience his repressed wishes. He therefore is not concerned about what might occur if he were to pay attention to them. He will have such concerns only after the analyst has encouraged him to pay attention to his repressed wishes. If the analysand can come to appreciate the analyst's purpose in offering an interpretation that has the aim of lifting repression, he will then elaborate in his mind various ways of responding to the expectations raised by the analyst's interpretative activity.

An analyst, for example, might suggest to an analysand who is devaluing his other analysands that he is envious of his relationship with his other patients but is finding it hard to experience his feelings of envy. In return, the analysand may elaborate in his associations his expectation of how the analyst might respond if he were to experience and acknowledge to the analyst that he felt envious of his other patients. Inevitably, here the analysand will be concerned about experiencing and observing his repressed feelings of envy.

The "alert" analyst, after offering this interpretation, listens to his analysand's associations and evaluates the effect his interpretive activity has had on him. He is looking for indications that the analysand has perceived his interpretation about his envy as tactless or critical. He is sensitive to allusions that show that the analysand has considered but rejected the notion of telling the analyst that he had hurt his feelings. More significantly for the present discussion, however, the analyst is trying to determine the conditions under which the analysand is willing to become engaged in the analytic work of lifting repression. This analysand is not imagining and then rejecting ways, in Friedman's terms, "to make [the analyst] do one thing or avoid another." The analysand is instead imagining the conditions under which he might be willing to meet the analyst's expectations that he lift his repression. The analysand, in offering his associations, is in effect negotiating with the analyst. He is attempting to ascertain whether the analyst himself is willing to provide the conditions and the kind of understanding that would mitigate his concerns. The allusions manifest in the analysand's associations indicate his tentative ways of working out with the analyst the conditions under which he would be willing to lift his repression.

I believe that this is a more complex but in many respects more accurate way to listen to the analysand's associations than that advocated by Gill and Friedman. In the approach I am highlighting, the analyst considers the likelihood that the analysand has appreciated his intention in offering his interpretation but that he is nonetheless reluctant to become involved in the analytic work until the analyst indicates his willingness to help the analysand tolerate his repressed feelings. This approach focuses more on the negotiations between analysand and analyst that are a prerequisite for lifting repression than on the source of the analysand's anger and the potential effects of this anger on the analyst.

Admittedly, this approach is not as readily applicable to the actual clinical situation as is Gill's. This is in part because I have been emphasizing an interactive process in which each participant listens to and is then influenced by the responses of the other party. In this situation the analyst first encourages the analysand to experience and observe his repressed wishes. When the analysand realizes what the analyst expects of him, he communicates his concerns to him. The analyst in turn listens for indications of the concerns the analysand manifests in his associations and then acts in a way that he hopes will enhance the analysand's willingness to lift his repression. This is a more complex and at times more ambiguous consideration of the analytic associations than one whose purpose is to remove the disguise from an imagined action as yet unexpressed.

In the instance where the analyst suggested to the analysand that he felt envious of the analyst's relationship with his other patients, the analysand might talk in the next session about a friend whose wife had divorced him because of his anger at her. From Gill's and Friedman's perspective, the analysand might have been angered by what he felt to be the analyst's criticism of his envious behavior. He might also be fearful of expressing this anger lest he be further chastised or even abandoned by the analyst. The analyst who holds this view might attempt to clarify this sequence of events in a way that gives the analysand permission to express directly his resentment toward him. If the analysand does so—if he decides "to make him do one thing or avoid another"—he will have had a corrective emotional experience, but he will not have lifted the repression of the more archaic aspects of his anger and his envy.

I believe that an analyst who follows the point of view I have been advocating and who aims at helping the analysand lift his repression would view this sequence differently. If the analysand believes himself to be criticized, the analyst would first consider the possibility that the analysand is basically unaware of the type of analytic work he is expected to accomplish in lifting his repression. He might indicate to the analysand more explicitly than he had done previously that it would be useful for him to allow himself to pay attention to the ways he experiences his repressed wishes. In so doing, the analyst would be encouraging the analysand to lift repression rather than merely giving him permission to express his anger at him.

The analyst who accepts my approach would then consider the possibility that the analysand is in fact aware of what he is expected to accomplish in lifting repression but has concerns about doing so. He would view the analysand's stated concerns about his friend's being abandoned by his wife to be more an allusion to his reluctance to be involved in lifting the repression of his envy than an indication of unexpressed anger at the analyst.

In this situation the analyst would consider the analysand as negotiating with him and would respond to him as someone who is actually attempting to work out the conditions under which he would be willing to lift the repression of his envious feelings. An analysand who is negotiating with the analyst in this manner is likely to be concerned about whether the analyst appreciates his efforts to cooperate. The analyst who overlooks and does not respond appreciatively to the analysand's attempts to involve himself in the work runs the risk of confusing the analysand. An analysand may react to an intervention aimed at having him express his inhibited anger as if the analyst were unwilling to help him tolerate his repressed envy. But in the propitious situation where an analyst shows his appreciation of the analysand's effort to negotiate the conditions under which he would be willing to lift his repression, he is more likely to mitigate one of the more significant concerns the analysand has about becoming involved in the analytic work. Here the analysand's awareness that the analyst does appreciate his efforts to lift repression is apt to enhance his willingness to continue with the work.

3 The Analyst's Interference with the Lifting of Repression

In the previous chapters, I have described the effect of the analysand's childhood interactions with his parents on his potential for lifting repression as an adult. I have suggested that an analysand whose early interactions have resulted in his employing more global and primitive defenses than repression will have great difficulty responding to a classical approach that encourages him to pay attention to and accept responsibility for the archaic aspects of his instinctual wishes.

Yet the failure of an analysand to participate successfully in a classical analytic approach may not result solely from a lack of early helpful dialogues with his parents. In this chapter I shall explore the role of the analyst in promoting or interfering with the lifting of repression. If the analyst is unaware of what is involved in the process of lifting repression, even an analysand who has the potential will not accomplish this work. Before the analysand can become willing to enter into what Freud has called "this school of suffering," the analyst must first highlight, often in specific terms, the importance of his actually experiencing and paying attention to the archaic aspects of his desire and anger. Once the analysand has realized what he is expected to do, the analyst should address and attempt to mitigate the analysand's inevitable concerns. Moreover, when the process has become firmly established, the analyst needs to allow it to deepen and must not interfere in ways that preclude the analysand from experiencing the affective components of his instinctual wishes. If the analysand is to gain optimal benefit from his analysis, the analyst should avoid overemphasizing reality-testing. An analysis is not likely to progress if the analyst fails to make it clear to the analysand that it is necessary for him to pay direct attention to his instinctual feelings or if he fails to address his analysand's reluctance to do so.

There are various reasons why an analyst may avoid following this course. Some analysts minimize the significance of lifting repression and advocate another therapeutic approach instead. They may highlight measures that seek to raise an analysand's self-esteem or further his ability to test reality. Although these measures are obviously indicated in many analytic situations, some of the self-psychologists and followers of the British school of object relations appear to downplay the significance of lifting repression, even in instances where the analysand is primarily manifesting evidence of neurotic conflicts.

There are other analysts who consider it valuable to lift repression but are not clear about what is involved in this process. They therefore do not take the steps necessary for enhancing the process or may interfere with it once it has begun to develop. Often the analyst's failure to promote the process is secondary to his countertransference. The analyst himself is in a vulnerable position when he encourages an analysand to experience archaic aspects of his instinctual wishes, for he is likely to be concerned about the intensity of these wishes toward him. He may become anxious to a degree that interferes with his objectivity. Under these circumstances he will overlook his analysand's concerns about engaging in the process, and the analysand in turn will feel misunderstood and react in ways that anger the analyst. The analysand may criticize the analyst or devalue what he is pointing out. In reaction the analyst may confront the analysand with his lack of cooperation or "interpret" the unconscious source of his resistant behavior in an increasingly insistent manner. These measures interfere with rather than enhance the analysand's willingness to pay attention to how he experiences his repressed wishes.

Ralph Greenson has presented a vivid illustration of this type of interaction in his article "Loving, Hating, and Indifference towards the Patient."[1] Greenson recounts a situation in which he had told his analysand that he experienced her complaining as "painful." He asserts that his countertransference was responsible for his critical remark to her. The transaction Greenson describes resonates with experiences all psychoanalysts have had. I believe, however, that Greenson does not focus in sufficient detail on the process that eventuated in his outburst. He does not recognize that his analysand had been reacting resentfully to his earlier failure to ascertain how to help her lift repression.

Countertransference refers to the analyst's response to a reaction his analysand is having toward him. The analyst may be unaware that he is responding in this manner, as when he does not realize that he is affected by his analysand's erotic feelings for him. He may be aware of his response but unclear about the basis for it, as when he becomes angry in response to his analysand's devaluation of him. His countertransference is likely to interfere with his capacity to conduct the psychoanalysis.

Greenson was sufficiently angry at his analysand to let her know that her "nagging and complaining" behavior was painful

1. Ralph Greenson (1974), Loving, Hating, and Indifference towards the Patient. *Int. Rev. Psycho-anal.* 1, pp. 259–266.

for him. He obviously was aware that he was angry at her, but we do not know what he identified as the source of his anger. At some point during their interchanges, it appears likely that he became irritated by her unwillingness to develop a transference neurosis or to show appreciation of his efforts to help her. His increasing irritation culminated in his making a critical remark.

However, the crescendo of insistent interpretative activity and defiant manifestations of resistance that Greenson describes was secondary to his earlier failure to mitigate the analysand's concerns about lifting repression. Because of this failure, the analysand remained unwilling to place herself in the vulnerable position of paying attention to and acknowledging her erotic feelings for him. Instead, she expressed anger at him because she felt he wanted to entice her into this vulnerable position, and he in turn became angry at her because, to his mind, she was refusing to be psychoanalyzed.

This reaction raises the question of why Greenson had failed to address his analysand's concerns about acknowledging her feelings to him. Later in this chapter, I will describe a situation in which I believe the analyst's failure to do so was owing to his failure to appreciate fully the importance of mitigating a reluctance of this nature. It is likely that Greenson did recognize the need to frame interpretations in a manner that would enhance the analysand's capacity to comprehend their meaning. In this instance, nonetheless, some type of countertransference response interfered with his usual ability to present his interpretation to his analysand in a way that promoted the process. It is possible to infer that Greenson's countertransference was already affecting his analytic work at the point when he first attempted to offer an interpretation and long before he made his angry statement to the analysand. Greenson himself notes:

> After an initial phase of loving and sexual feelings to me, she embarked upon a long period of complaining, fault-

> finding, thinly disguised contempt for my work and the lack of progress. Many interpretations of her hostility to me, her unconscious envy, the defense against her loving feelings, her wish to provoke sadistic or angry reactions in me, were to no avail. In one hour, after much complaining and fault-finding, she paused and unexpectedly said, "I guess I am no pleasure to work with." (p. 260)

Greenson admits to having had to restrain himself from making a sarcastic remark to her and replied instead, "Yes, these hours of nagging and complaining and complaining and nagging are a pain" (p. 260). He believed that what he called his "confrontation" had a salutary effect in ameliorating the analytic stalemate that had existed for some time. He discusses at considerable length his conviction of the therapeutic efficacy of his statement in spite of the fact that it represented a "countertransference reaction."

The analysand's own words following Greenson's confrontation indicate that her complaining was a reaction to her sense that he was insensitive to her concerns about experiencing and acknowledging her erotic feelings for him. Greenson reports:

> She then proceeded to talk about how her nagging and complaining was like a buffer zone, keeping a distance between us. Actually she often felt a feeling of rejection by me from the way I analyzed her sexual and romantic feelings earlier in the analysis. She now realized she hated me for this, envied my composure, and "half-consciously" decided to keep me at a distance, disparage me, and tease me by her constant complaining with the expectation that she would break down my "God-damned indifference." (p. 264)

This sequence of events suggests that the analysand had begun to feel erotic and romantic feelings toward Greenson earlier in the analysis. She was sufficiently aware of what she was experiencing to acknowledge these feelings to him. However, Greenson had discussed these feelings in a way that caused her to feel rejected. I assume that Greenson understood the importance of her paying active attention to the way she experienced her erotic feelings for him. I am also assuming that the analysand had some understanding of the type of analytic work he was expecting her to accomplish.

Greenson's way of interpreting interfered with rather than enhanced the analysand's willingness to become involved in the lifting of her repression. It is not apparent from the case report whether the analysand directly voiced her concerns about placing herself in the vulnerable position of experiencing her repressed desire toward her analyst. But she herself clearly states that she often felt rejected because of the manner in which Greenson had analyzed her sexual and romantic feelings toward him. This suggests that there might have been another way for Greenson to have encouraged her to experience and acknowledge her erotic feelings about him that would not have caused her to feel as rejected as she did. It is likely that if Greenson had been more alert to her concerns about lifting repression and had attempted to address them, she would have been more willing to engage in the analytic process. Her hesitancy to continue with the work turned into a more organized type of resistance when she realized that Greenson was ignoring her concerns. At that point she decided to "keep [him] at a distance, disparage [him] and tease [him]." I am suggesting that this decision resulted more from her sense that he was "indifferent" to the risks she feared would develop in lifting repression than from her feeling that he did not reciprocate her emerging desire for him. His insensitivity to her precluded her from taking the risk necessary for lifting repression. It also gave her a reason to disparage his therapeutic acumen.

The clinical material Greenson describes points to an important analytic issue: why an analyst in this position fails to address the concerns his analysand has about experiencing and acknowledging his or her erotic wishes for him. This failure most often occurs when the analyst feels anxious and vulnerable about becoming the object of his analysand's desire and anger. It is further compounded when the analyst has a narcissistic, if defensive, need to be in complete charge of the analytic process.

Before Greenson's analysand finally succeeded in breaking down his resistance, Greenson reacted to her disparagement of him in a manner that compounded her reluctance to experience and acknowledge her repressed wishes for him. At this point Greenson was not empathic to his analysand and was unaware of what was causing her to disparage him. He was now reacting to her reaction to his earlier failure to address her concerns. He was trying rather frantically to force her to accept the one right "interpretation" of the unconscious "wish" that he held to be at the basis of her resistance. He did not recognize that under these circumstances she would be incapable of experiencing her hostility, her unconscious envy, her defense against her longing feelings, or her wish to provoke sadistic and angry feelings in him in a way that would be of use to her. Moreover, at this point he did not consider how he might enhance her willingness to experience and observe the feelings associated with the "wishes" he was "interpreting" to her. He was unaware of her "half-conscious" decision to break down his indifference. In effect, he insisted that she overcome her resistance, and he made his interpretations in a way that was destined to be ineffective and counterproductive. Under these conditions she could only perceive his interpretations, whatever their validity, as further proof of his indifference.

The analysand's efforts to keep Greenson at a distance can be considered as indications of a refusal to involve herself in the analytic work. Yet from a more salutary and long-range view, her behavior represented an effort on her part to induce him to provide the conditions under which she would be willing to continue with the work. In disparaging and teasing him, she was not only keeping a distance between them but also endeavoring to make him more sensitive to the feeling of helplessness she experienced when she tried to pay attention to her desire for him. Her unexpected remark, "I guess I'm no pleasure to work with," shows that she was aware that her actions might alienate him, but she also hoped that they would lead him to give some tangible indication not that he desired her but rather that he would help her tolerate her desire for him. In fact, she became more willing to become involved in the analytic work after he discussed with her what had been going on between the two of them.

Frequently the analyst, the analysand, or both may be considerably less clear about what must occur if the analysand is to lift his repression than I have assumed to be the case with Greenson and his analysand. Of course, the analysand will not be aware of the importance of his paying attention to what he actually experiences if the analyst himself does not think about the process of lifting repression in these terms. If he does not, the analyst may anticipate that the analysand will respond to his interpretations cooperatively and acknowledge their validity without experiencing the affective aspect of the repressed wishes. In this situation the analyst is unaware of the importance for the analysand first to experience aspects of his repressed wishes and then to pay attention to what he has experienced in meaningful ways. He fails to delineate the nature of the analytic work involved in lifting repression. The analysand becomes confused about what he is trying to do and feels helpless in the face of the feelings that have been evoked by his interactions with the analyst. He may show his confusion about what the analyst is expecting of him and be asking the analyst, directly or indirectly, to clarify the nature of the analytic work. By contrast, Greenson's analysand more or less understood the nature of the analytic work but doubted the analyst's willingness to be helpful if she were to become involved in it.

A relatively inexperienced analyst sought consultation with regard to a young female analysand who he claimed was responding to his interpretations in a "highly resistant" fashion. He believed that her dreams and associations suggested an erotic transference to him. But when he attempted to interpret this to her, she responded in either a noncommittal or a confused manner. His interventions evoked complaints—about her employers, her husband, and the analysis—rather than useful associations. She did not present him with what he considered to be a "meaningful view of her inner life."

The analyst was disconcerted because the analysand did not appear to be deepening her understanding of herself. He was particularly distressed because she would frequently report her dreams at the end of her sessions and did not leave him enough time to make an interpretation. He stated that he had a countertransference reaction to her and acknowledged that he felt "provoked by and irritated at her." He had thought about pointing out to her what he felt were the underlying hostility and seductiveness of her provocative behavior. He also had considered confronting her with "the detrimental effect" that her unwillingness to cooperate with him was having on her analysis. He did not act on these ideas because he felt that for him to do so would seem to her as if he were scolding her and would be counterproductive.

The analysand had recounted to him two typical dreams at the end of successive analytic sessions. In the first dream she said that she was trying to elicit "some kind of response" from a male employer. In her dream she felt excited in an unusual way that was hard for her to describe. When the employer did not respond, she became "disappointed." In the next dream she was being criticized by an older woman. These and similar dreams suggested to the analyst that she was manifesting an erotic transference. But whenever he attempted to talk to her about her feelings for him, she would either stop dreaming for a while or would report her dreams just as the session was ending. The analyst felt that the fact that she presented complaints rather than associations that he might interpret indicated a need to be withholding. He felt that her offer of accessible material only at the end of the session showed a wish to tease him.

The analyst responded to the analysand as if she clearly understood what he was expecting of her. Yet, it appears that he himself in this situation was far from clear about the nature of the analytic work involved in lifting repression. He acted as if all that was necessary for the work to be accomplished was for her to listen to his interpretations and cooperate by accepting as valid what he pointed out to her. He believed that she had decided not to cooperate and had chosen instead either to withhold her associations or to present them in a manner that would provoke and tease him. He thought about "overcoming her resistance" by exposing what he felt were the hostile and seductive motives responsible for her behavior.

Her responses to his interventions, moreover, indicate a marked lack of understanding on her part about the nature of the analytic work. I believe that she did not realize what he wanted her to do when he discussed her erotic wishes. Presumably she had developed some erotic feelings for him, but she did not know what she might make of them. She was unaware of the purpose of acknowledging these feelings to him and how it might be of value to her to pay attention to them.

An analysand who recognizes what type of analytic work he is expected to accomplish when he is offered an interpretation is usually reluctant to lift repression until his concerns about doing the work have been addressed. In attempting to mitigate these concerns, the analyst helps the analysand distinguish the analytic situation from the original childhood one in which he had needed to repress instinctual wishes. By contrast, the analysand I have just been discussing had not been helped by the analyst to realize in what ways the analytic situation differed from the childhood one.

In one of the dreams she reported to him, she stated that she experienced disappointment when she was unable to elicit "some kind of response" from a male supervisor at work. It is highly probable that in elaborating and then reporting this dream to her analyst, she was alluding to the disappointment she had been experiencing with him in the analytic situation. The fact that in her dream she felt excited "in an unusual way" that was hard for her to describe suggests that she was vaguely aware of experiencing erotic reactions toward him. Moreover, the dream in which she was criticized by an older woman suggests that she had been anxious and guilty about experiencing these feelings. The analyst interpreted her dream as an indication that during her oedipal period she had been disappointed by her father's failure to respond to her and had felt her mother to be critical of her for her forbidden desires. It is quite probable that a similar type of disappointment and sense of being criticized were evoked by her emerging transference reactions toward her analyst. At this stage of her analysis, however, the critical intervention would be to clarify the nature of the analytic work rather than to interpret her oedipal issues. I believe that to tell her that she was disappointed in her analyst because he had not reciprocated her desire for him would only have intensified her confusion and her sense of being criticized. She required a response from him that would indicate the purpose to be served by her paying attention to and then acknowledging what she was experiencing.

Undoubtedly the analysand's actions and the content of her dreams were overdetermined. Her tendency to report her dreams at the end of the analytic hour was influenced by one or another of the various unconscious conflicts that Greenson attributed to his analysand in his insistent efforts to overcome her resistance during their stalemate. It is possible that the particular dream under discussion was the manifestation of this analysand's cautious but not conscious effort to ascertain whether the analyst would recognize and respond positively to her disguised acknowledgment of her desire for him. But without a clear sense of what to do with her erotic feelings once she experienced them, she did not know how to make use of interpretations that addressed either a hypothetical unconscious motive for the late reporting of the dream or the latent meaning of the dream's manifest content. His suggestion that she was asking him whether he reciprocated her desire for him would only have added chaos to confusion. Before this type of intervention could be helpful to her, she would have to understand clearly the purpose of experiencing and acknowledging her desire for him.

The particular interventions contemplated by this analyst—namely, confronting the analysand with the detrimental effects of her resistance or interpreting her hostile motives for her withholding actions—would not have enhanced her willingness to observe her erotic feelings. The most appropriate response from him at that point would have been one that clarified for her the value of experiencing and observing her repressed desire. Whether an analyst should illustrate this purpose in great detail is problematic. It should be recalled that Freud offered the Rat Man an elaborate explanation of how he would benefit from entering "this school of suffering." Yet there are occasions when this strategy would dilute the affective component of the analysand's experience to the point where there would be little meaningful to observe. Nonetheless, an analysand is not likely to pay attention to what he is experiencing unless he has been helped to acquire some idea about why doing so might be of use to him. In spite of the fact that her disappointment in the dream alluded to her unreciprocated desire for the analyst, it would have been more appropriate to regard it as an indication of her sense that the analyst, in his role as supervisor, had failed to "teach" her something about what she could do with her erotic feelings. From this perspective, her primary motive in reporting her dreams at the end of the hour was neither a wish to tease him nor a tentative inquiry about whether he reciprocated her desire. Rather, her disappointment was a reflection of her uncertainty about how the analyst would respond if she were to ask for help in clarifying what she might do about her feelings. It was as if she was wondering out loud why he did not assist her in making sense out of the "exciting" feelings she found so hard to describe.

The analyst in this case did not have a clear notion about the nature of the analytic work he was asking the analysand to accomplish. He was unaware that she herself was uncertain what she was to make of the erotic feelings emerging into her consciousness. As a result, he did not clarify for her the purpose and value of allowing herself to pay attention to these feelings. Often, however, the analyst's own anxiety about how he himself might react to the analysand's acknowledgment of her feelings for him is responsible for his failure to offer clarity. The analyst might become anxious and guilt-ridden if he were to experience erotic feelings toward his analysand, and this reaction is likely to be exacerbated if the analysand acknowledges her erotic feelings for him. More often, the analyst protects himself from the angry reaction that he anticipates from the analysand because he cannot reciprocate her desire. In some instances an analyst may protect himself from experiencing the sadistic pleasure that would arise from being in a position to reject the analysand's desire for him.

Whatever its source, an analyst's anxiety will interfere with his ability to enhance the analytic process. It will limit his empathy for his analysand and his recognition that the analysand is uncertain how to proceed. Because of his own anxieties the analyst cannot appreciate the vulnerable position his analysand is in when she experiences intense feelings for him without having a frame of reference in which to place them. As a result, he is apt to put pressure on the analysand to "resolve" her transference neurosis before she has actually developed one. He will insist that she validate the "meaning" of his interpretations as a way of protecting himself from experiencing his own unacceptable feelings.

In an analytic situation where both parties have a basic understanding of the nature of the analytic work to be accomplished, the analyst has succeeded in indicating the purpose and benefits of lifting repression. In order for the analysand actually to become engaged in this process, it is also necessary that the analyst address the analysand's concerns about experiencing and observing archaic aspects of his desire and anger. A working alliance is established when these two conditions are fulfilled. Establishing such an alliance is difficult. For a long period of time the analyst and the analysand are motivated by divergent goals. Moreover, it is sometimes only after an unusual strain or crisis in the analytic relationship that the analyst and the analysand become capable of collaborating. Even where a working alliance appears to be well established, the analyst may at times intervene in an insensitive manner. He may insist that the analysand relinquish his "resistance" to paying attention to his feelings. In this case the working alliance is disrupted more by the analyst's confrontation than by the analysand's reluctance to become engaged in the analytic work. The analysand then becomes increasingly unwilling to experience and observe his feelings about the analyst and may justify his reluctance by focusing on what he experiences as the analyst's insistent and critical attitude.

In this situation the analysand's anger arises more from his sense that the analyst has failed him as an analyst than from the fact that his desire is not being reciprocated. The analysand may express this anger through unwillingness to involve himself in the type of analytic work that the analyst expects him to accomplish. He may experience sadistic pleasure in the analyst's discomfort in failing in his role as analyst. In any case, here the analysand is retaliating for the analyst's failure to be of help to him by frustrating the analyst's need to be perceived as helpful. In turn, the analyst may insist that the analysand recognize and renounce the behavior that appears to him to be sadistic. In this mutually antagonistic state of affairs the analysand will not be able, let alone ready, to pay attention to his sadism, even though it may motivate his withholding behavior. Moreover, at that moment, the analyst himself is incapable of offering an interpretation in a way that might be useful or of considering whether something other than an interpretation is called for. Yet where a firm alliance has been established before this regressive series of events takes place, both parties, even as they appear to be interacting nonproductively, may be searching for ways to repair the relationship. Each of them may become aware that his own neurosis is interfering with the alliance and may look for means to establish a rapprochement that will allow the analytic work to continue.[2]

At the start of her analysis a young woman told her analyst that she "knew" she was expected to fall in love with him and have sexual feelings for him. She said that she was unwilling to do this, however, because it would be humiliating for her to be involved in a one-sided relationship. During the early phases of her analysis the analyst suggested that aspects of her dreams indicated that she had more feeling toward him than she was aware of or was willing to acknowledge. She said that although this was possible, she was not going to allow herself to be enticed into a position where her affection would not be reciprocated.

The analyst attempted to address her concerns about plac-

2. Paul G. Myerson (1973), The Establishment and Disruption of the Psychoanalytic *Modus Vivendi*, *Int. J. Psycho-Analysis* 54, pp. 133–142.

ing herself in this vulnerable position. But after he suggested that it would be useful for her to acquire a fuller understanding of what she was experiencing, he did not put pressure on her to become more involved in this aspect of the analytic work. In response, she elaborated some aspects of her reluctance to pay attention to and acknowledge to him what she was experiencing. She said she enjoyed her fantasies and was afraid that if she were to tell him about them, she would lose an important source of pleasure. She also described a traumatic situation in her childhood in which she was humiliated after telling a relative that she loved him. She recalled that at the time she had resolved never again to place herself in a position where she would be hurt in this way.

During the course of a five-year analysis she became less reluctant to talk about her fantasies but refrained from describing their sexual details. The theme of the fantasies that she reported reflected an important aspect of the way she actually related to the analyst. A man who resembled the analyst would propose to her that they run away together. Sometimes she would decide to go with him, but only after telling him that their relationship would not be a permanent one. Sometimes she would tell the man that although she was pleased that he wanted to elope with her, it was in both of their interests for her to decline his proposal. She came to realize that the themes of her fantasies recalled the way she had limited her involvement in the analytic work.

In spite of her recognition of this similarity, she continued to restrict what she revealed about her sexual fantasies. Occasionally she reported conversations she had had with other women about their sexual experiences and fantasies. The analyst suggested that in reporting these conversations, she might be referring to her own sexual issues. She did not openly agree with this suggestion. One time she did acknowledge that she had sexual fantasies involving the analyst but stated that they were "none of his business." The analyst did not insist that she tell him details about her fantasies because he believed that this would increase her anxiety and intensify her reluctance to do other aspects of the analytic work. He reasoned that by allowing her to make her own decision about how explicit she was to be in divulging the details of her sexual fantasies, rather than urging her to say everything that was on her mind, he would hear more about her inner life in the long run. Moreover, her analysis appeared to be progressing favorably. She had become more aware of her envy and her competitive wishes. Her increased awareness of aspects of her instinctual wishes was associated with a lessening of her depression and an increase in self-confidence. She was more successful at work, and for the first time in her life she had established a meaningful relationship with a man. Nevertheless, the analyst wondered if his "permissiveness" might have been a rationalization for timidity. He realized that he was somewhat angry at her for acting in what he felt to be a controlling manner. Yet he was on guard against expressing his anger. He was particularly alert to any impulse he might have to insist that she "confess" the details she was reluctant to reveal. As a result, he did not confront her and instead attempted to help her increase her awareness of herself.

Nonetheless, several times he rather abruptly shifted from encouraging her to pay attention to her feelings and reactions to insisting that she behave differently in the analysis. One of these occasions occurred after she had reported her reactions to hearing a senior officer of the organization she worked for criticize a man with whom she was competing for a promotion. She had earlier indicated her dislike of this colleague. Her pleasure in relating the event was obvious to the analyst. He believed that her guilt about this kind of sadistic pleasure had contributed to her chronic feelings of depression and to her inhibition at work and in her relationships. He suggested to her that she was taking more pleasure in her colleague's discomfort than she was aware of and that both her enjoyment of her competitor's disgrace and her discomfort in becoming aware of this enjoyment were "natural" reactions. The analyst realized that he was talking to her in an unusually solicitous manner. He was also aware that his solicitude revealed his own discomfort in highlighting her pleasure in hearing about someone else's disgrace.

Her initial reaction to his remarks was to justify her anger at her colleague. She then became depressed and talked about herself in a deprecatory way. In turn, the analyst suggested that her self-criticism indicated that she felt guilty about experiencing pleasure in her rival's downfall and that this type of guilt was a significant factor in her depression. His discomfort about highlighting her sadism led him to tell her that she was "unnecessarily" feeling guilty about her reactions.

His reassuring remarks, both before and after she became self-critical, reflected his anxiety about the pain he might be inflicting on her. It should be remembered that from time to time he was aware of feeling irritated by her unwillingness to involve herself in what he considered to be significant aspects of the analytic work. His irritation may have been compounded by her reluctance to acknowledge that she had involved him in her erotic fantasies. His legitimate reasons for interpreting her sadism gave him the opportunity to vent his less legitimate anger at being rejected by her. He was preconsciously aware of his anger, and his reassuring comments showed that he was attempting to contain it.

During the next session she informed him that even if what he had said to her the day before was correct, it was of no use to her. She emphasized that he was especially "off the mark" in saying that she was unnecessarily feeling guilty about the pleasure she took in another person's discomfort. In fact, she said, she was "a really bad person whom no one could possibly like." At this point the analyst experienced the analysand as rejecting him by devaluing his efforts to help her understand more about her depression. He ceased considering feelings, either his or hers, and confronted her with the detrimental effects of her behavior. He told her forcefully that he thought she really knew what he was getting at when he clarified the connection between her experiencing pleasure in a colleague's disgrace and her subsequent depression and that she was telling him she was bad in order not to recognize this relationship. In effect, he was no longer encouraging her to pay attention to what she was feeling but was now insisting that she behave more compliantly and accept his clarification.

His outburst had a predictable effect. She started the next session by telling him that she was "now really angry at him." She said he had "no right" to talk to her in such a critical manner. But even while she was criticizing him, the analyst did not feel that she was seriously angry. He sensed, in fact, that she was rather pleased at having goaded him into responding in other than a therapeutic way. Later in the session she said she would like to know what she had done to make him angry. After the previous session the analyst had wondered why he had confronted her so unempathically and had reflected on the source of his annoyance. He recalled that at times he had been irritated because of her refusal to involve herself in the analysis in a way that would replicate her childhood neurosis. He realized that on several occasions he had experienced her as taking pleasure in withholding her fantasies from him. He had been aware that he himself at times had reacted to her withholding behavior by experiencing sadistic feelings toward her. He had tried not to express his anger toward her but also had been atypically reassuring when he had previously pointed out the connection between her sadism and her depression. Upon further reflection, he was struck by the fact that he had confronted her immediately after she had indicated that she did not appreciate his efforts to help her recognize what caused her depression.

It was clear to both parties that he had been angry. The analyst believed that a rapprochement could not occur until he acknowledged that he had played a significant role in their regressive interaction. During the next session he told her that he had been irritated because he felt that she had not permitted him to help her. He reviewed with her their interactions during the past several days and highlighted the discrepancy between their views about why she had become depressed. He reminded her that she had not accepted his suggestion that she was depressed because of her guilt about the pleasure she took in her rival's discomfort. He told her that he had wanted to help her become more tolerant of her anger and that when she said that his remarks were not helpful and that she was really a bad person, he perceived her as criticizing his efforts to help her. He had come to realize that he had overreacted to her criticism of him and had therefore defensively confronted her with her own reluctance to accept his perspective about her depression. He also said that between sessions he had been thinking about the reasons for what had taken place.

The analyst did not go on to tell the analysand that he had been annoyed at her for some time because she had not revealed her fantasies to him, nor did he acknowledge that he had experienced sadistic feelings toward her. He believed that her state of mind was such that she could not appreciate an interpretation that highlighted her pleasure in having caused him to have lost his composure. Moreover, he thought that she would become confused and upset if he told her he had been angry because she had withheld her feelings and fantasies from him.

She became pleased and thoughtful after the analyst offered these revelations. She said she appreciated what he had told her. The analyst felt that her pleasure at this point was quite different from the triumphant enjoyment she had experienced following his earlier confrontation. In the next session she recalled childhood events that provided considerable insight into her reluctance to become more open and direct with him about her feelings. She remained reluctant to reveal the details of her fantasies but was able to experience and acknowledge the pleasure she derived from frustrating the analyst's wish for her to reveal them to him.

In this episode both the analyst and the analysand were relatively clear about the nature of the analytic work the analysand was expected to accomplish. The analysand, however, had directly indicated her reluctance to do this work. On a number of occasions the analyst had attempted to address her concerns about becoming more involved. He had become angry at her limited involvement in the analytic process. His anger was indirectly manifested in the atypical reassurance he had given her when he pointed to her pleasure in hearing someone else criticized. A mutually reinforcing regression developed. His anger and his guilty efforts to contain it interfered with his ability to enhance whatever willingness she might have had to lift her repression. He apparently needed evidence from her that he had helped her develop insight into herself to counteract his guilt about pointing out aspects of her sadism. However, she perceived his "interpretation" of her sadism as an attack and a criticism. In this frame of mind she was unwilling to remain allied with him in furthering her insight. Moreover, she apparently took this opportunity to frustrate what she had sensed as his need to be of help to her. In turn, he felt criticized and devalued, and he retaliated by insisting that she take what he was saying to her at face value.

The rapidity with which they recovered from their regression reflects the care and consideration with which the analyst had earlier addressed the analysand's concerns about accomplishing the analytic work. Recall that I suggested that Greenson's analysand disparaged him in part to induce him to act more sensitively. Greenson's willingness to acknowledge that he had been insensitive appeared to be a prerequisite for her willingness to become involved in the analytic process. Perhaps something similar occurred in the situation I have just described. That analyst clearly felt disparaged when his analysand told him that he was being of no use to her. But his willingness to acknowledge to her that he had been angry and to discuss some of the reasons for his anger helped reestablish the alliance necessary for the analysis to progress. Her pleasure in realizing that her disparagement had upset the analyst had made her uneasy. She was eager to restore the therapeutic relationship once she recognized that the analyst himself was also eager to resume his analytic role.

4 Therapeutic Approaches

In the previous chapters I argued that an analysand's ability to lift repression during a psychoanalysis presupposes his involvement with a parent in relatively helpful dialogues about the sexual and aggressive feelings he experienced during his oedipal period. Such dialogues not only helped divert the child's attention from the more archaic aspects of his instinctual wishes but also helped direct it to related yet less conflicted and potentially manageable feelings and actions. As a consequence of these dialogues, the child is presented with a view of what is happening and especially of what might happen that counters his sense of catastrophic helplessness. This view enhances his ability to relate in satisfying ways and promotes his sense that he is an active agent who is able to pay attention to and accept responsibility for important aspects of his sexuality and anger.

An analysand who has been fortunate enough to have been engaged in this type of dialogue will generally anticipate that the analyst intends to be helpful. However, inasmuch as the analyst is encouraging him to experience, and to direct his attention toward, the very feelings and fantasies his parents had originally helped him direct his attention away from, the analysand will be reluctant to accomplish the analytical work of lifting repression. Yet because his early dialogues with his parents were helpful, he will have enough confidence in the analyst's intentions to realize that he can acknowledge his concerns to the analyst and to anticipate that the analyst will respond constructively. If the analyst, for his part, finds the right way to address the analysand's concerns, the analysand will be willing to attempt to lift his repression.

There are many people who do not use repression as a primary or even a major mode of defense. By and large, these people have not had helpful interactions with their parents at times of stress in early childhood. Faulty parent-child interactions during the pre-oedipal period reduced the likelihood that helpful dialogues would take place when the child experienced heightened libidinal or aggressive wishes toward his parents. The child discovered that he could not anticipate that his parents would be understanding and helpful if he let them know what he was feeling on those occasions. He came to realize instead that he would be left helpless with these feelings or would be criticized for having them. Parents who did not foster their child's efforts to individuate or who discouraged his attempts to be intimate are unlikely to have been willing to help him find compatible ways of tolerating and coping with significant aspects of his libidinal and aggressive wishes. In fact, they may have been so unresponsive in their dealings with the child that later in his life he distrusts the idea of talking about what he is feeling.

A person with this kind of background has not been helped to use repression in the way I have been describing and therefore does not have access to it as a primary defense. He resorts to other defenses, such as denial, projection, and splitting, which restrict his awareness and limit his abilities to cope with inner and outer realities in more extreme ways than does repression. When he attempts to relate, he is likely to have much more anxiety than someone who uses repression as his major mode of defense. He may or may not be more severely "ill" than the more neurotic type of individual. Guntrip functioned more adequately than the Rat Man. However, someone who does not use repression will not develop a sense of himself as an active agent who accepts responsibility for his instinctual wishes.

It is difficult, if not impossible, to engage a person with this background in the kind of analytic dialogue I have been elaborating. As an analysand, he will distrust the idea of talking about his feelings because his parents' disregard for them made it unconstructive or perhaps even destructive for him to express them. He lacks the sense that the other person in a dialogue will have the capacity or motivation to help him find meaningful ways to tolerate significant aspects of his desire and anger. He is, of course, suffering considerable anxiety about what he is feeling and wants someone to help him alleviate his suffering. Yet because of his early detrimental experiences with his parents, it is hard for him to see how discussing his feelings will lead to anything other than abandonment or criticism. This analysand is likely to be confused when the analyst attempts to lift repression. He will not provide the associations the analyst expects, or he will insist that the analyst is not being helpful and will reject the notion that he is "responsible" for what he is feeling. He may appear to the analyst to be withholding, demanding, and manipulative.

These reactions are best viewed as secondary to his confusion. He is confused because the analyst expects him to lift repression, a goal that has no relevance for him. His willingness to engage in treatment will depend on the analyst's capacity to focus more accurately on the source of the analysand's difficulty. If repression is not the primary problem, it is not appropriate to attempt to lift it. In this situation the analysand is best served if the analyst takes another approach.

Having said this, I should make a distinction between

individuals for whom the lifting of repression is the wrong approach and those for whom it is appropriate but who at times during an analysis become reluctant to engage in the process. It is a rare analysand who never complains that the analyst is not being helpful or who never externalizes. Where the analyst does not address his analysand's concerns about lifting repression, even an analysand for whom the lifting of repression is a meaningful approach may temporarily withdraw from the analytic work. When Greenson did not address his analysand's concerns about engaging in this work, she withdrew from the process and began to find fault with him. He eventually realized that something of this nature was underlying her resistance and modified the way he applied his approach, although he did not change it. In response, she involved herself in the work, and he was in a position to help her lift the repression of her instinctual wishes. This situation differs from one in which an analyst comes to believe that the analysand's persistent complaining, externalization, and regressive behavior indicate that the lifting of repression is not meaningful and subsequently decides to change his approach.

In the last several decades both the British school of object relations and self-psychologists have described approaches to therapy that are quite distinct from the one that aims at helping the analysand lift repression. These approaches, to speak in general terms, have as their purpose to help the analysand relate to others in more comfortable and satisfying ways rather than to help him become aware of his repressed wishes. The analyst who applies this type of approach holds that the analysand's version of events is more or less valid rather than viewing it largely as a distortion. This analyst will encourage the analysand to separate from old and limiting modes of relating in order to risk new and more intimate ones. He interacts with the analysand as an available person who is offering him the opportunity to undo the constrictions resulting from the past unavailability of the analysand's parents. The analyst, when he conducts this type of analysis, accepts the analysand's anger as a natural reaction to the people who have failed him. The analyst expects that his own humane and steadfast behavior will help the analysand realize that it is possible to individuate and to relate more intimately without losing a meaningful connection with a significant person in his life. The analyst does not primarily engage the analysand in the kind of dialogue that has as its basic purpose to enlarge the analysand's awareness of his repressed wishes. Instead, the analytic interaction is a corrective emotional experience that enhances the analysand's ability to change his behavior and way of relating.

In this chapter I will make use of Heinz Kohut's paper "The Two Analyses of Mr. Z" (1979) to elaborate how the dialogue or lack thereof significantly influences whether a classical or a nonclassical approach is the more appropriate one for conducting a psychoanalysis. During his first analysis of Mr. Z, Kohut considered the analytic material entirely from the view of a classical analysis. Unlike Greenson, Kohut changed his approach rather than the way he applied it during his second analysis of this analysand. He states that in the second analysis "I relinquished the health-and-maturity morality that had formerly motivated me, and restricted myself to the task of reconstructing the early stages of his experience, particularly as they concerned his enmeshment with the pathological personality of the mother" (p. 12). At the point where Kohut changed his approach, he no longer viewed his analysand as capable of lifting repression, "as resisting change or opposing maturation because [he] did not want to relinquish [his] childhood gratifications, but on the contrary, as desperately—and often hopelessly—struggling to disentangle [himself] from the noxious selfobject, to delimit [himself], to grow, to become independent" (p. 12).

In the first analysis Kohut had expected that Mr. Z, "with the aid of analytic insights that would enable him to see his past clearly, [would] relinquish his narcissistic demands and grow up" (p. 12). Kohut indicates that during the early stages of this first analysis the analysand behaved in a grandiose manner, and his "narcissistic demands" were very much in evidence. However, "during the early part of the analysis his grandiosity and his narcissistic demands had been taken up and were worked through, both in so far as they were the continuation of his fixation on the pre-oedipal mother and in so far as they were clung to as a defense against oedipal competitiveness and castration fear" (p. 8). He also noted that Mr. Z opposed his interpretations with "intense resistances" (p. 5). Kohut writes that his analysand reacted negatively to the statements about his narcissism and "blew up in rages against me time after time—indeed the picture he presented during the first year and a half of the analysis was dominated by his rage" (p. 12).

It is important to emphasize that during the first analysis Kohut considered his analysand as a "centre of independent initiative" (p. 12)—what I am calling an active agent. If he were correct, the analysand would have expressed a conscious fantasy indicating incestuous desire for his mother and competitive rivalry with his father before he had found it necessary to repress them. Kohut believed that his analysand's demanding behavior showed his unwillingness to pay attention to his incestuous and competitive wishes. This view is evident in Kohut's interpretations stressing the defensive nature of the analysand's grandiosities: "I interpreted the persistence of defensive narcissism as it protected him against the painful awareness of the powerful rival who possessed his mother sexually and against the castration anxiety to which awareness of his own competitive and hostile impulses towards a rival would have exposed him" (p. 6).

During the first analysis Kohut responded to Mr. Z as though the analysand was able to cooperate in the analytic work of lifting his repression but was unwilling to do so. He notes that he experienced Mr. Z as "resisting change" and "opposing maturation." These statements suggest that Kohut considered him to be aware of what he was expected to accomplish: first to relinquish the childhood gratification of being catered to by a doting mother and then to pay attention to his incestuous and competitive wishes. Kohut viewed Mr. Z as stubbornly refusing to give up his pre-oedipal gratifications from his mother and to come face to face with his conflicted desire and anger toward her.

In the early phases of this analysis Kohut attempted to overcome what he perceived as Mr. Z's unwillingness to do the analytic work. He states that he confronted his analysand's "demands that the psycho-analytic situation should reinstate the position of exclusive control, of being admired and catered to by a doting mother who . . . had, in the absence of siblings who would have constituted pre-oedipal rivals and, during a crucial period of his childhood, in the absence of a father who would have been the oedipal rival, devoted her total attention to the patient" (p. 5). Kohut told his analysand that this demand would not be fulfilled in the analytic situation and insisted that Mr. Z relinquish his hope that he would achieve it. In short, he made it clear that if Mr. Z wanted to have a meaningful relationship with him, he would have to "grow up" with "the aid of analytic insights" (p. 12). I believe that Kohut's emphasis on his analysand's unwillingness to accomplish the analytic work, coupled with his insistence that he overcome his resistance, was the behavioral manifestation of the "health-and-maturity morality" that Kohut came eventually to recognize characterized his attitude toward his analysand during the first analysis.

In my view Kohut was in a predicament that was somewhat similar to the one in which Greenson had earlier found himself. In both situations the analysts viewed the analysands as able but unwilling to do the analytic work of lifting repression. Moreover, both analysts attempted to overcome the analysands' unwillingness to do this work by confronting them with the detrimental effects of their reluctance. Their insistence that their analysands relinquish their supposed unwillingness interfered for a long time with the analysts' own ability to consider why the analysands were not engaged in the expected analytic work.

Mr. Z's difficulty, unlike that of Greenson's analysand, was due not to his reluctance to lift repression but to his inability to do so. The material Kohut presents suggests that Mr. Z had not been afforded the opportunity to engage in helpful dialogues as a child and therefore had not employed repression as a primary mode of defense. During the time that Greenson was insensitive to his analysand, she refused to cooperate. Yet once he changed the way he applied his approach, she paid attention to the way she experienced her repressed wishes. Kohut likewise insisted that his analysand involve himself in the analytic work of lifting repression. As he subsequently realized, however, Mr. Z's early interactions with an extremely intrusive and controlling mother and the nonavailability of his father invalidated his assumption that the analysand was striving to recapture the gratifications of his first years. It had not been possible to have helpful dialogues with such parents. If Mr. Z was struggling to disentangle himself from his mother and needed Kohut to help him in this struggle, it was inevitable that he would be confused and distressed by an analyst who kept talking about the gratifications of a doting mother and about becoming aware of his incestuous desires toward her.

Although both analysands reacted to their analysts' interpretations in a complaining, critical, and devaluing manner, there was, I believe, a fundamental difference in the states of minds that underlay their actions. Greenson's analysand apparently understood what he expected her to do—that is, pay attention to her repressed desire. But she "often felt rejected by the way he had analyzed her sexual and romantic feelings towards him" (Greenson 1974, p. 264) and stopped cooperating with him. The analysand may have begun to complain actively as a means of avenging herself on him for what she considered to be his unempathic attitude. She may even have hoped that her complaining would force him to address her concerns. In any case, she was capable of recognizing the type of work he expected her to accomplish but unwilling to cooperate with him until he showed more appreciation of her vulnerable position.

By contrast, Kohut was insisting that his analysand, who was still enmeshed with an intrusive and controlling mother, recognize that he wanted her to gratify his dependent wishes and reciprocate his more phallic ones. Mr. Z was being asked to accomplish something he was incapable of doing. Whatever desire he had for his mother was submerged by the anger, guilt, and helplessness her behavior had evoked in him. Moreover, she had been totally unavailable to help him understand what he was experiencing about her. Even though he himself was not clear at the time about what he needed from his analyst, he was angry at him for insisting that he do something that was impossible. He was only aware that what the analyst was offering was of little value to him. He needed first an accurate understanding of his feelings toward his mother and then the opportunity to separate from her. At the time, his analyst was not offering this mode of empathic understanding and help. Mr. Z's complaining reflected his considerable distress about Kohut's failure to understand him, and he used it in a desperate attempt to get him to change his approach to his emotional difficulty. Greenson's analysand complained in part to take revenge on an analyst whose way of going about the analysis led her to feel humiliated. Kohut's analysand complained to let him know that treatment was not working and to plead with him to find a more helpful approach. As long as Kohut was locked into his "health-and-maturity morality" and the approach that went with it, he was unable to do so.

Kohut himself thought the changes in his analysand's behavior during the second half of the first analysis "had come about as the direct result of the mobilization and the working-through of Mr. Z's nuclear conflicts" (p. 8). Toward the end of Mr. Z's first analysis Kohut "consistently, and with increasing firmness, rejected the reactivation of his narcissistic attitudes, expectations, and demands by telling the patient that they were resistances against the confrontation of deeper and more intense fears connected with masculine assertiveness and competition with men" (p. 8). At this time Kohut was convinced that "the patient seemed indeed to respond favourably to this consistent and forcefully pursued attitude on my part" (p. 8). Although Kohut recognized in retrospect that the termination phase of the first analysis was "emotionally shallow and unexciting," he says he was "surprised when, about four and a half years after the termination of his analysis, Mr. Z let me know that he was again experiencing difficulties" (p. 9).

In the second analysis of Mr. Z, Kohut made a conscious decision to change his approach. He now viewed Mr. Z's relationship with his mother in an entirely different light. He no longer considered Mr. Z to be yearning for her as the object of either pre-oedipal or oedipal desires. Moreover, he did not view his analysand's petulant and angry behavior as an indication that he was frustrated or conflicted over these desires. Instead, he understood that Mr. Z was seeking to be liberated from his extremely intrusive and controlling mother, not to possess her. His mother had not wanted him to lead a life separate from her and had hindered his individuation. His father had been quite unavailable and of almost no use in whatever efforts Mr. Z had made in the past to disentangle himself from his mother.

Because his mother allowed Mr. Z so little distance from her, he had not become aware of how intrusive she actually was and of the effects of this intrusiveness on him. He had idealized his mother and had not recognized her unempathic attitude toward him. As Kohut points out, "The mother's emotional gifts were bestowed on him under the unalterable and uncompromising condition that he submit to total domination by her" (p. 13). During the first part of the second analysis Kohut confronted the analysand with his mother's limitations. He notes that Mr. Z's associations revealed "the emergence of gradually deepening insights into the essence of his relation with the mother, above all his recognition of the serious distortion of the mother's personality which determined the nature of their relationship" (p. 13). Kohut also helped Mr. Z recognize that his intense resistance toward and anxiety over becoming aware of the real nature of his relationship with his mother were related to his fear of losing his attachment to her. He reports that Mr. Z feared "the loss of the mother as an archaic self-object, a loss that, during this phase of remembering and working through the archaic merger with the mother, threatened him with dissolution, with the loss of his self that at these moments—and there were more than moments—he considered to be his only one" (p. 13). In other words, Mr. Z had idealized his mother and denied her intrusiveness in order to maintain a connection with her that he believed was the only condition under which he could survive and not fall apart.

Kohut discusses his efforts to help Mr. Z disentangle himself from his unhealthy attachment to his mother:

> After the slow and painful process of freeing himself from the idealized outlook on his relation with the mother had gone on for some time, enabling him for the first time to recognize that the section of his self that had remained merged with her since childhood was neither all of himself nor even its central part, he began haltingly, and against surges of severe resistance motivated by disintegration anxiety, to talk about some of the mother's most overtly abnormal activities when he was a child and adolescent. (p. 14)

Kohut encouraged the analysand to become aware of his mother's difficult and intrusive qualities and then to realize that he could survive independently of her. He was in effect telling Mr. Z that his mother had acted against his welfare and, most significantly, that he himself considered Mr. Z to be intact enough not to need her.

There is clearly a difference between the types of interventions Kohut offered Mr. Z during his two analyses. In the first analysis Kohut tried to help Mr. Z pay attention to his repressed desire and anger so that he might understand himself more fully and "grow up." In the second analysis he intended to help Mr. Z recognize the unhealthy characteristics of his mother so that he might separate from her. Kohut's conclusion that his analysand lacked the potential to observe and tolerate the threatening and archaic aspects of his desire and anger led him to employ a more direct mode of intervention. In so doing, he promoted the analysand's identification with him as a means of helping him to become aware of his mother as a "noxious selfobject" and to separate from her and establish new modes of relating.

Kohut's change in approach correlates with the way he viewed the analysand's masochistic masturbatory fantasies in the two analyses:

> Specifically, as far as he could recapture the masturbatory fantasies, they were always more or less extensive elaborations of themes taken from *Uncle Tom's Cabin*, a book which Mr. Z's mother had read aloud to him on numerous occasions during his childhood years, either at bedtime or when he was ill. In the fantasies which occurred invariably from age 5 to age 11 he imagined himself a slave, being bought and sold by women and for the use of women, like cattle, like an object that had no initiative, no will of its own. (p. 6)

In the first analysis Kohut considered these fantasies to be a source of pleasure and Mr. Z's masochism to be a "sexualization of his guilt about his pre-oedipal possession of his mother and about his unconscious oedipal rivalry" (p. 7). He tried to convince Mr. Z that his image of a phallic woman had the purpose of denying the castration anxiety he would experience if he were to become more aware of his repressed desire for his mother.

In the second analysis Kohut "realized not only that neither his masturbation nor his involvement in the primary scene had ever been enjoyable, but that a depressive, black mood had pervaded most of his childhood." Kohut now believed that the masturbation was Mr. Z's attempt, "through the stimulation of the most sensitive zones of his body, to obtain the reassurance of being alive, of existing" (p. 17). He no longer felt that Mr. Z obtained gratification and pleasure through the elaboration of a fantasy in which he played the role of slave. He now believed that Mr. Z used the fantasy to sustain himself and to tolerate the displeasure of being enslaved by his mother.

These perspectives call for different approaches. In his original formulation of Mr. Z's psychopathology, Kohut considered that Mr. Z had enough of a center of independent initiative to have experienced conscious desire for his mother and to have wished to remove his father from the scene. During the analysis Kohut apparently believed that when Mr. Z became anxious and guilty about experiencing these wishes, he retained the capacity to desire and to be assertive even as he repressed the more primitive aspects of his instinctual wishes. This view suggests that Mr. Z remained capable of elaborating a fantasy in which he could experience derivatives of his archaic desire in a manner that was still gratifying. But to understand Mr. Z's fantasy as Kohut at first did, it is necessary to assume that he had had a relatively healthy dialogue with his mother during his childhood.

It is conceivable, although unlikely, that when Mr. Z's mother read *Uncle Tom's Cabin* to him, she had his welfare in mind and was trying to enhance his ability to relate to the world in satisfying ways. She might have been attempting to divert his attention from his highly conflicted fantasies toward her, including those that involved his freeing her from his father's bonds, toward less threatening, more manageable ones in which he bravely rescued the downtrodden. Yet Kohut's increasing awareness of the actual nature of Mr. Z's relationship with his mother eventually convinced him that she "had by no means been in empathic contact with the needs of his self for an anticipatory resonance to its future power and independent initiative" (p. 14). This idea leads to the conclusion that there had been no actual dialogue between Mr. Z and his mother. In all probability she read him the novel to force her own fantasy on him. She failed to help him individuate and relate successfully to other people. Kohut and Mr. Z realized that Mr. Z's mother "had always taken totally for granted that, however great his successes in life, their relationship would never be altered, he would never leave her" (p. 14). In this context his mother's reading him *Uncle Tom's Cabin* conveyed to him the inevitability of his continued status as a slave.

Kohut no longer believed that it would be possible for Mr. Z to lift the repression of his pre-oedipal and oedipal desire for his mother. He abandoned his view that Mr. Z could obtain derivative gratification through the elaboration of a fantasy in which he played the role of a slave. In the second analysis he related to and interacted with Mr. Z as if he were actually enslaved by his mother and needed to free himself from her.

Kohut states that during the first part of the second analysis he restricted himself to reconstructing the early stages of his analysand's experiences, particularly as they concerned his enmeshment with his mother. It should be emphasized that Mr. Z's actual liberation from his mother—even his beginning awareness of the real nature of his mother's personality—was achieved only with great difficulty. As Kohut says:

> The emergence of his memories, . . . and especially his acquisition of gradually deepening insights into the es-

> sence of his relation with his mother, above all his recognition of the serious distortion of the mother's personality which determined the nature of their relationship, was accompanied by great anxiety, often leading to serious resistances. The flow of his revelations would then be interrupted and he retreated from the pursuit of the analytic task, voicing instead serious doubts whether his memories were correct, whether he was not slanting his presentation to me. (p. 13)

Kohut thought that behind Mr. Z's denial of his mother's noxious characteristics, the analysand himself wanted to separate from her. He encouraged Mr. Z in this endeavor and voiced confidence in his ultimate capacity to succeed. Kohut made heroic efforts to counter Mr. Z's disintegration anxiety and resistances that developed in the course of effecting this separation.

I believe that it would not have been possible for Mr. Z to "disentangle himself from the noxious selfobject, to delimit [himself], to grow, to become independent" if Kohut had confined himself to indicating in a neutral manner what Mr. Z's mother was really like and how she affected him. Mr. Z was, as Kohut puts it, "struggling" to free himself from his mother's unhealthy hold on him even though his impetus to struggle was largely unexpressed. He needed an analyst who could articulate what he was going through and who could identify with him and encourage him as he struggled to individuate. Kohut prompted his analysand's identification with him and indicated the positive values of separation, growth, and independence. He states that the crucial moment in the second analysis occurred when "for the first time now—and with a glow of happiness, of satisfaction—Mr. Z began to talk about positive features in his father's personality" (p. 19). Mr. Z's recall of these positive aspects of his relationship with his father shows the strong identification he had established with Kohut. In the first analysis Kohut had insisted that his analysand renounce a pleasurable attachment to a desired mother. In the second analysis he struggled along with Mr. Z to counter the dangers of leaving a familiar but crippling attachment to his mother as well as to face the risks inherent in unfamiliar but potentially satisfying new relationships.

In the first analysis Kohut had interacted with Mr. Z as if the analysand had repressed his instinctual wishes but was unwilling to lift repression. He had forcibly urged him to relinquish his supposed pre-oedipal attachment to a doting mother and pay attention to the oedipal desire that he was purportedly experiencing toward her. Kohut's insistence had kept him from recognizing that his analysand's confusion and despair were due to his being asked to accomplish a type of analytic work that was impossible for him.

The apparent success of Mr. Z's second analysis and Kohut's account of the stifling effect of his mother on his individuation give credence to the correctness of Kohut's decision to change his approach. His observations and his reasoning confirm one of the fundamental hypotheses I have been setting forth—namely, that the presence of relatively healthy dialogues in childhood is a prerequisite for lifting repression during a psychoanalysis. Kohut's analysand did not appear to have engaged in such dialogues with his parents and accordingly was incapable of lifting repression. For the purpose of drawing general principles from this case material, however, we should consider the unlikely possibility that during his childhood Mr. Z might have had healthier dialogues with his parents or a nursemaid than Kohut has indicated and that the analyst's anxiety about dealing with certain of the analysand's repressed wishes led him to change his approach. I have suggested previously that the analyst's own vulnerability may preclude him from adequately helping an analysand who does have the potential to lift repression. There are instances where an analyst changes his analytic approach because of the anxiety he experiences while he is encouraging his analysand to lift repression rather than because of a correct reappraisal of his analysand's personality structure. When an analyst is analyzing someone who has certain of Mr. Z's characteristics, he might become anxious about addressing the sadistic elements of the analysand's repressed wishes. If the analyst were to realize that he is anxious and to look for the cause of it, he would be in a position to seek the means to address the analysand's concerns about lifting the repression of his sadism.

In the first analysis Kohut attempted to analyze Mr. Z's anger in terms of his competitive and hostile impulses toward his father. He apparently did not encourage Mr. Z to pay attention to the intense anger he felt toward his mother over her failure to return his love. It is hard to escape the conclusion that someone in Mr. Z's position would be angry at his mother, though consciously he may not have experienced this anger. A mother such as Mr. Z's would be incapable of recognizing and then reciprocating his wish to be loved as an autonomous individual, and accordingly she would reject his wish to be viewed as separate and independent from her.

Kohut has stated that Mr. Z found it extremely difficult to disentangle himself from his mother because of his fear of disintegrating in the process. But it remains possible that on some of the occasions in his childhood when he experienced sadistic feelings toward his mother, he might also have become engaged in a healthy dialogue with her or another adult caretaker that enabled him to repress his sadism rather than employ a more primitive defense against it. As a consequence, his need to cling to his mother in adult life may have been due to the guilt he would have felt had he allowed himself to experience pleasure at her distress over their separation.

In theory, at least, Mr. Z might have profited greatly if Kohut had encouraged him to pay attention to his sadistic feelings toward his mother instead of attempting to help him separate from her. He may himself be reluctant to assume responsibility for a son's separation from his mother. The analyst may realize that what he views as a useful disentanglement is from the mother's perspective an abandonment. Under these circumstances he would be hesitant to enhance his analysand's awareness of the sadistic pleasure he would experience if he were to cause his mother pain through separating from her. Moreover, it is likely that the analyst would be fearful about becoming the object of the sadism he is trying to interpret. These concerns may motivate him to select an approach that allows him to play the role of a good father helping his son escape from the bondage of an intrusive and controlling mother.

An analyst faced with the stagnation of an analysis similar to the one described in this chapter should address both of the issues I have pointed to in my discussion. He should ask himself whether he is attempting to promote a classical psychoanalysis with an analysand whose early dialogues were not compatible with the employment of repression. The analyst should also keep in mind that his own anxiety about the consequences of interpreting his analysand's repressed wishes may be motivating him to change his approach. An experienced analyst, familiar with this dilemma, is aware that it is often hard to draw a definite conclusion about these issues. Nonetheless, only through careful consideration of them can an analyst further his understanding of the analytic process and determine the most useful way to proceed in the analytic situation.

5 The Treatment of Narcissism

In chapter 4 I addressed the reasons an analyst may decide to stop using an analytic approach designed to lift the repression of instinctual wishes. His decision may be based on recognition that the analysand's personality structure precludes him from becoming aware of the archaic aspects of his desire and his anger. The analyst may conclude that the nature of the analysand's interactions with unavailable or unempathic parents did not enhance his use of repression as a major defense. In that situation the analyst appropriately recognizes that to continue his efforts to encourage that analysand to lift repression would be an exercise in futility.

By contrast, an analyst may decide to change his approach when a change is not necessary. He may not realize that it is essential for him to promote the conditions under which the analysand will become willing to lift repression. He may be unaware that it is crucial for the analysand to understand clearly the type of analytic work he is expected to accomplish. Moreover, the analyst may not appreciate the necessity for him to address the various concerns the analysand will have about lifting repression. In some instances the analyst's own responses to the unfolding of the analysand's internal feelings toward him may make him anxious and motivate him to change his approach.

There are certain situations where practically all observers would agree with an analyst's conclusion that the analysand's personality structure makes it impossible for him to profit from a classical analytic approach. Arnold Rothstein has described two analyses of severely disturbed narcissistic personalities whose early interactions with their mothers interfered with the type of development that would allow them to respond to a classical approach:

> It seems reasonable to hypothesize that throughout Mr. M's first eighteen months of life he was exposed to a chronic traumatic developmental process wherein his active seeking of fusion experiences was met with cold unavailability or angry rejection. In response he withdrew and through a variety of self-stimulating modes sustained himself. This process was probably associated with a premature and fragile integration of his self-representation. In contrast, Mr. G was exposed to a traumatic developmental process characterized by inconsistency. His mother was unempathically overstimulating or unavailable for his phase-appropriate attempts at fusion and the elicitation of affirmation. The maternal inconsistency may have contributed to the fluidity of the regressive potential characteristic of the integration of his self-representation.[1]

Under these circumstances neither patient as a child could have carried on the type of dialogue that I have suggested is the prerequisite for employing repression as a primary defense.

In cases such as Rothstein describes, a classical analysis is

1. Arnold Rothstein (1982), The Implications of Early Psychopathology for the Analyzability of Narcissistic Personality Disorders, *Int. J. Psycho-Analysis* 63, pp. 177–188.

clearly out of the question. There are instances, however, where the complexity of the clinical material makes it difficult for the analyst to determine whether to use a classical or other approach. I consider Heinz Kohut's decision to change his approach toward Mr. Z to be based on solid clinical grounds. But in elaborating general conclusions drawn from his case material, I expressed reservations about the necessity of this step. The fact that most analysands have had both helpful and unhelpful interactions with their parents during their development contributes to the complexities of appraising such a decision.

Clinical experience shows that most analysands present both neurotic and narcissistic features. In previous chapters I have indicated that an analysand's helpful dialogues with his parents enhance his ability to employ and to lift repression. Where an analysand has been involved in less healthy interactions with a parent, he has found it necessary to use more global and primitive defenses than repression, and the use of these defenses is concomitant with the development of a narcissistic orientation. It is critical to determine whether a major change in the analytic approach is always required in instances where the analysand manifests well-developed narcissistic features. An analyst who is faced with this dilemma may sometimes achieve more for his analysand by modifying his approach than by changing it radically.

Charles Hanly describes the analysis of a woman whom he treated in a classical manner.[2] He maintains that his use of what he refers to as specific therapeutic interventions to modify aspects of her narcissism was not incompatible with his carrying out a classical analysis. Hanly viewed the narcissistic features of his analysand as secondary to her difficulties in her libidinal and aggressive interactions with her parents rather than as the out-

2. Charles Hanly (1982), Narcissism, Defence and the Positive Transference, *Int. J. Psycho-Analysis* 63, pp. 427–444.

come of, in Kohut's (1971) terms, "a separate line of development." In fact, he presents the exposition of this case as "an experiment with the resources inherent in the classical theory for understanding and treating the narcissistic features that complicate neurosis" (Hanly 1982, p. 438). In this instance the analyst found a way to modify the narcissistic features of the analysand without changing his approach.

Hanly postulates the existence of a "narcissistic defense," which he argues "serves to render unconscious the experiences of narcissistic injury *and* the aggressive impulses animated by the rage provoked by them" (p. 434). According to Hanly, this defense serves to keep the individual's attention away from both feelings of anger and the events that activate those feelings. The defense is likely to develop under circumstances where the parents have injured the child's narcissism and have not appreciated the fact that his feelings have been hurt. As a result, they fail to find ways to help him cope with his reactive anger. Hanly is apparently discussing situations where the parents on occasion have been responsive to their child's state of mind. If the parents have sometimes appreciated that the child's feelings have been hurt and have been successful in talking to him in a caring way, he will have the sense that people may intend to be helpful when he is experiencing distress. This sense makes it more probable that he would benefit from a classical analysis. But if the parents fail the child on most occasions, he will present problems in maturing and will be incapable of making use of a classical approach.

Hanly's analysand had a reasonably healthy relationship with her mother under many conditions. However, she was narcissistically injured at the anal stage of her development. According to Hanly, "a fastidiously anxious mother had failed to take any pride in the accomplishment of the patient's bowel and instead had demanded an acquiescence in adult standards of cleanliness and regularity before the abandonment of the auto-erotic anal pleasures could be rendered tolerable by the child's developing capacity for object love" (p. 434). In Hanly's view, this mother's failure to "take pride" in her child's "accomplishment" had narcissistically wounded the child and intensified her anger. We can only assume that the analysand had not had the kind of helpful dialogue with her mother that might have enabled her to find ways to express the less archaic and more manageable aspects of the instinctual wishes evoked during toilet training. The mother's demands for acquiescence would have frustrated whatever efforts the child herself might have made to initiate this helpful dialogue. As a result, the analysand had developed narcissistic modes of functioning that interfered with her recognition that her feelings had been hurt and that she was angry at the people who had hurt her. Instead, she became preoccupied with concrete objects that offered her narcissistic and autoerotic satisfaction. Hanly reports that the analysand became "extremely house-proud and lavished great attention and care upon the furnishing of her home" (p. 433). In addition, he maintains that her narcissistic behavior served as a way of getting back at those people who frustrated or did not appreciate her various needs. Thus she would berate her husband, with whom she was quite competitive, "if he was careless enough to place his suitcase on the bedspread while packing it for one of his scientific trips" (p. 433).

Besides the narcissistic aspects of her character, Hanly states that the analysand manifested "a rather classical hysterical neurosis exacerbated by external events in [her] life history" (p. 433). He reports that the most devastating external event in her life had been her parents' divorce when she was eleven, which led to her father's abandonment of her. Hanly suggests that this trauma had intensified her anger toward men. He adduces evidence that points to the analysand's wishes for revenge and to her penis envy. Hanly demonstrates that her eventual ability to tolerate and become aware of the feelings and fantasies associated with these reactions helped her overcome the marked sexual inhibition that was present at the start of her analysis.

Hanly conducted his analysis in an essentially classical manner. His success in enhancing the patient's ability to lift repression suggests that in spite of the analysand's childhood traumas, her parents were at times available enough to engage with her in dialogues that made it possible for her to employ repression. Moreover, she was fortunate enough to have encountered an analyst capable of recognizing and addressing her concerns about becoming involved in this type of analytic work. In my view, the specific therapeutic interventions Hanly used to modify his analysand's narcissistic features are variants of the responses an analyst needs to make to mitigate an analysand's concerns about lifting repression.

In the early part of her analysis Hanly's analysand had manifested several types of resistance. She was frequently silent and often upbraided the analyst for neglecting her. Hanly reports that she also "developed intense anxiety on Sunday evenings in anticipation of Monday sessions and would plead with her husband to insist that she terminate her analysis" (p. 432). Hanly goes on to elaborate his dilemma in finding the best way to understand and manage this resistance:

> I took the view that the patient's third early transference symptom [her Sunday anxiety] was being caused by her unconscious expectation that I would either abandon her as her father had or subject her to punishing silences of my own after the fashion of her mother. The problem was that there were often few indications of the unconscious identification at work in the transference. At the same time, I sensed that too much watching and waiting on my part could result in an impasse. Accordingly, I regularly made interpretations of her defenses followed up by clarifications of

> the feeling states that maintained them: fear of the intensity of her anger, helpless rage, fear of my withdrawal, rejection or abandonment, fear of yet another narcissistic humiliation at my hands from which she wanted her husband to protect her by terminating her analysis. (pp. 432–433)

Accordingly, it appears that the analysand was concerned that if she did reveal to Hanly her feelings, particularly her angry ones, he would abandon her or punish her. His interpretations and clarifications reflected an effort to mitigate these concerns and demonstrate that he was trying to help her make sense out of what she was experiencing. It should be noted that Hanly did not interpret her silence as being motivated by a wish to get back at him or destroy his therapeutic endeavors. Rather, he considered it a way to protect herself from a repetition of traumatic situations in which she had felt rejected and humiliated. Perhaps that is why Hanly, unlike Greenson, promoted the analytic work instead of provoking the analysand to keep him at a distance.

Hanly indicated that his analysand reacted to his interpretations and clarifications "with a mixed feeling of relief and fear that [he] understood how she was feeling" (p. 433). She was no longer silent and now revealed many aspects of her feelings, including her sadistic reactions to men. The vicissitudes of her early development had not kept her from being able to distinguish between situations where someone is attempting to be helpful to her and those where someone is trying to control and humiliate her. The analysand's capacity to distinguish between helpful and unempathic interventions suggests that her narcissistic features resulted from her efforts to defend herself against the temporary failure of her parents during stressful periods of her childhood, rather than indicating a pervasive inability to trust and relate to other people.

Later, Hanly again intervened in a way that served at least

as much to mitigate the analysand's concerns about involving herself in the analytic work of lifting her repression as it did to modify her narcissistic features. Prior to the intervention the analysand had become more aware of certain aspects of her sadistic fantasies, particularly those that appeared to be manifestations of her penis envy. This awareness coincided with more adequate functioning, but the improvement did not carry over into her sexual life. Hanly reports that she again became silent; this time, however, her "silences had a sad, depressive quality but they did not suggest anger." She began to "report dreams in which she *found herself standing alone in front of a large house, or in the country with a mountain behind her, or on the seashore with a high promontory overlooking the beach*" (p. 436). Hanly notes that "these dreams were largely pleasurable, despite the fact that in connexion with them she would dismay herself with the thought that they expressed the wish to leave her husband and to live alone." He goes on to state:

> Interpretations to the effect that she was not alone in the dream and that the large house, the mountain and the promontory had some other significance not yet apparent to her eventually led to a crucial transference fantasy. It turned out that on a Sunday outing she had arranged to drive past my house. In the fantasy I was an old man, living in the house alone. She imagined visiting me, bringing wood for the fire, and food. She imagined sitting quietly for hours without speaking, basking in the warmth of the fire and of my undivided, adoring attention. It was this fantasy that was unconsciously determining her new transference silences. Notwithstanding the function of that fantasy as a denial of oedipal conflicts, it appeared to me that the fantasy was also an attempted reparation of the narcissistic injuries already examined above [the traumatic toilet training and the abandonment by her father]. It gave

> expression to a positive transference of the narcissistic type described by Kohut. Interpretations governed by the perception-surmise issued in a powerful affective response of rueful grief. [The analysand] began to mourn not only the loss of her father but the loss of the experiences of the lack of confirming love that she had wanted from both parents during her earliest childhood. (p. 436)

Hanly maintains that his analysand was employing her fantasies as a means of repairing her narcissistic injuries and compensating for the losses she had experienced in her childhood. He emphasizes in his discussion that her fantasy of basking by the fire and having his undivided attention gave her narcissistic satisfaction. Undoubtedly, as he states, this aspect of her fantasy was a manifestation of a "narcissistic mirroring transference." In addition, her fantasy of taking care of him is evidence that she also wished for a relationship that was mature rather than exclusively self-centered. Presumably the way Hanly interacted with her when he interpreted what she desired from and with him validated both wishes as legitimate ones for her to have entertained. Her earlier silence suggests that she was concerned about how he would react to her if she were to tell him this fantasy. It is clear that once she revealed her fantasy, the way he interpreted it gave her the sense that he accepted her rather than being critical or rejecting of her wishes. Her ability to express these wishes to him and his salutary response to them were undoubtedly reparative and freed her to do the significant work of mourning the loss of her father and facing the fact that she had lacked love and caring from both her parents.

I am suggesting, however, that something even more fundamental than helping the analysand mourn her losses took place. By this point in her analysis the analysand was engaged in a dialogue directed toward helping her lift repression. Hanly underscores that the analysand's mourning was not "sufficient in itself" and that "its essential effect was to facilitate the release of the patient's object libido into her sexual conflicts" (p. 436). The analysand was becoming increasingly aware of the nature of the analytic work he expected her to accomplish, and to some extent she was already aware of the threatening, hostile, and sadistic fantasies that were about to emerge into consciousness in the analysis. Hanly reports that "one of these fantasies was having intercourse with a man, and achieved orgasm [*sic*] by taking a razor blade, slitting his throat, and watching the blood spurt out" (p. 437).

The clinical material shows that the analysand was experiencing sadistic fantasies even before she reported the fantasy indicating that she desired Hanly's undivided, adoring attention. Thus the analysand's silences, which occurred before she reported her pleasurable dreams, demonstrate her resistance to reveal her sadism as well as her hesitation about acknowledging to Hanly that she had positive feelings toward him. The analysand was undoubtedly concerned that the destructive nature of her fantasies would threaten her relationship with her analyst and cause him to react critically toward her. On the other hand, she recognized that if he were to be of help to her, she would have to pay attention to her fantasies and tell them to Hanly. Most likely she needed Hanly to indicate that he would not react negatively and that he would appreciate her efforts before she would become willing to lift the repression of her sadistic wishes. Viewed in this light, her fantasy of bringing him wood and food may have represented an indirect way of asking him how he would react if she were to bring her sadistic fantasies to the analytic situation. He had already pointed out that she was not "alone" in her dreams, and his later "perception-surmise" after she reported the transference fantasy highlights his availability to repair the damage caused by her early traumas. He had offered her clear signs that he would not be critical of her if she were to pay attention to and acknowledge whatever she might experience and that he would in fact be appreciative of her active involvement in lifting repression. In so doing, he mitigated her concerns and enhanced her willingness to involve herself in the analytic work.

Hanly describes his analysand's distress as her sadistic fantasies emerged and "as she struggled under the burden of the task of working through the impulses and affects that attended them" (p. 437). He too found this process distressing and states that "analysis would be emotionally intolerable work were it not for the fact that the removal of fantasies from repression does accomplish therapeutic work" (p. 437). This otherwise "intolerable work" did lead to a definite lessening of the analysand's sexual inhibitions. She lifted repression to the extent that she realized that elements of her behavior during her oedipal period had been motivated by "curiosity and love for her father's penis" (p. 437). Her increased awareness and tolerance of her instinctual wishes changed her relationship with her mother. She no longer viewed her as intimidating but established an affectionate relationship with her. Moreover, she was able to feel attracted to her husband.

In this analysis the therapeutic work associated with the lifting of repression led to a fundamental change and far-reaching outcome. The analyst and analysand established a relationship in which the analysand herself actively participated in this painful and rewarding work. Two elements were essential for this outcome that are generally not taken into consideration in discussions of the relationship essential for lifting repression. First, the analysand developed sufficient trust in the analyst to risk asking him whether he would appreciate her wish to cooperate with him and would remain available to her even if she were to expose disturbing aspects of her feelings. Second, the analyst indicated through his responses that he did appreciate the risk she was taking and that he would not be alienated by anything she might tell him about herself.

The analysand's traumatic toilet training had left her feeling narcissistically wounded and helpless to control her reactive rage. As a consequence, she did not readily trust people and was prone to retreat to a narcissistic position. Fortunately, she had had sufficiently healthy dialogues and interactions with her parents so that under the propitious conditions of her analysis with Hanly she was able to relinquish her narcissistic defense and become engaged with him in lifting repression.

It will be recalled that Hanly states that he presented this case material as "an experiment with the resources in the classical theory for understanding and treating the narcissistic features that complicate neurosis." I developed my own argument as an extension of Hanly's "experiment." He says that his analysand required specific therapeutic interventions in order to modify these features. I believe that those aspects of the analysand's behavior that Hanly delineates as narcissistic—her silences in the analytic situation, her wish to be adored as expressed in her reparative fantasy—were indications of her concerns about becoming involved in the work of lifting repression and that Hanly's responses represent successful means of mitigating those concerns. Hanly's experiment and my extension of it are feasible and plausible because his analysand's significant narcissistic features reflected reversible defenses rather than a major characterological deficit.

Some persons undergoing psychoanalysis present more marked and less easily reversible narcissistic features than did Hanly's analysand. Under these circumstances the analyst sometimes must change his approach or at least use measures other than those aimed at lifting repression. Such measures are directed at helping the analysand act in less narcissistic ways. For this to occur, it is necessary for the analysand himself to take an active part in modifying his narcissistic orientation. Rothstein's patients, for example, suffered a profound disturbance in their early relationships with their mothers. This difficulty precluded them from making use of a classical analysis in which "the role of insight gained through interpretation [results] in progressive integration and autonomy" (Rothstein 1982, p. 177). Nonetheless, Rothstein believes that these patients may profit from a therapeutic approach:

> Although identification with the "analyst-introject" is an important component of the process, it is not the unique characteristic of the mode of therapeutic action of the analytic endeavor. This emphasis is important because there are subjects who can accommodate to an analytic situation but whose analytic process rarely develops past the regressive internalization of the analyst as reparative narcissistically invested introject characteristic of the mid-phase process. These subjects may experience significant therapeutic benefit from such a relationship. However, where reparative or "transmuting" internalization gained in the nonverbal "mirroring," "holding" or "containing" ambience is the primary mode of therapeutic action, a therapeutic rather than analytic result has been achieved. (pp. 177–178)

In the process Rothstein describes, the analyst is not engaging his analysand in the work of lifting repression. Rothstein indicates that analysands with more narcissistic pathology may profit from the "mirroring," "holding," and "containing" aspects of their relationship with their analysts. But he appears to be suggesting that these analysands may not play an active role in what gets accomplished through this relationship. His term "regressive internalization" implies that the reparative effect occurs without the analysand's becoming actively involved in the analytic work; rather, he benefits through a passive introjection of the caring aspects of the analyst. I believe, however, that the analysand will need to participate actively if he is to make lasting gains. A narcissistic analysand plays an active role in the analysis when he moderates his unrealistic expectations. This will occur only if he comes to his own conclusion that his expectations are unrealistic and if he finds more realistic modes of satisfaction. As I pointed out in chapter 4, Mr. Z actively participated in the struggle that resulted in his emancipation from his mother. The narcissistic individual's failure to have had healthy dialogues with his parents in his childhood does not keep him from collaborating actively with his analyst in furthering his understanding of how significant aspects of his inner and outer reality are interrelated. An analysand's introjection of and identification with his analyst do not by themselves lead to this collaboration. Kohut promoted Mr. Z's identification with him in a manner that enhanced the analysand's ability to separate and function independently. Mr. Z became actively engaged with Kohut in these efforts to overcome his anxiety associated with leaving his familiar but crippling attachment to his mother and search for new and potentially fulfilling relationships.

William Meissner has described his treatment of a man who manifested with defined narcissistic features.[3] Meissner emphasizes the specific technical measures he used to help his analysand temper his narcissistic characteristics, particularly his unrealistic expectations. He does not, however, present as detailed or clear a view of the way he approached his analysand's neurotic manifestations.

Meissner's description suggests that there were neurotic components to his analysand's psychopathology:

> The attachment to his mother was expressed not only in terms of needy dependence and infantile clinging but had a strong oedipal cast as well. He remembered that when he was little, his parents used to lie in bed late on Sunday mornings. He used to get up and crawl into bed with them,

3. William W. Meissner (1985), A Case of Narcissistic Personality, *Journal of the American Psychoanalytic Association* 33, pp. 437–469.

> preferring to be close to his mother's body, which he felt was smooth, warm, and soft. On such occasions he was distinctly aware of the wish that his father would not be there and that he would have his mother all to himself. (p. 447)

Meissner states that the analysand remembered "masturbating in his mother's bedroom" and that "all these sexual wishes and fantasies about his mother left him feeling bad inside as though there was something ugly, sinful, and guilty in him" (p. 447). He presents evidence from his analysand's dreams that the analysand manifested oedipal competitive wishes in the transference:

> Gradually . . . the dreams began to assume a more aggressive quality, particularly one dream in which he was shooting rockets at the top of a skyscraper. The rockets became more and more powerful, more and more destructive, and the building finally toppled in ruins at his feet. He analogized looking up at the top of this lofty structure to his looking up at me from his lowly position on the couch and wishing he could somehow topple me, bring me down to his level so that he would not have to feel little, helpless, and inferior. His fear of aggression reflected the underlying oedipal wishes to eliminate his father—a wish that had come to frightening fruition [his father had died suddenly when he was ten]. His retreat to a position of small, weak, helpless childishness protected against the destructiveness of his aggressive impulses. (pp. 454–456)

The analysand's ability to express aggression in his dream and to draw an analogy between the content of his dream and a wish to "topple" his analyst indicates that he had achieved some awareness of his competitive wishes. But Meissner, in his discussion of the analysand's oedipal transference, notes that he had little capacity to tolerate this aggression and shortly would retreat to a position in which he thought of himself as a sickly, weak, and impotent victim. The analysand's tendency to retreat suggests that he had not developed the ability to tolerate and accept responsibility for his competitive wishes. Meissner emphasizes the way he approached the narcissistic aspects of his analysand's psychopathology and downplays his treatment of the analysand's neurotic problem. This makes it difficult to agree or disagree with Meissner's conclusion: "It was not until the oedipal ground had been sufficiently worked and the ambivalent conflicts adequately worked through that the narcissistic issues could be effectively approached and dealt with" (p. 459). It is possible that Meissner shifted to the analysand's narcissistic issues before he had adequately worked through his oedipal issues. I have described several reasons this shift may occur. In this instance the cause may have been that the analysand had a narcissistic orientation and had not employed repression to any significant extent.

In the early stages of his analysis the analysand was helped to separate from his intrusive, guilt-evoking mother, who had been depressed for many years since the death of her husband, and to mourn the loss of his father, whom he had idealized even though the father had been relatively unavailable to him: "Insofar as important narcissistic issues were tied up both in the patient's hostile-dependent resentment of his mother and in the mourning of the loss of his father, the success of the analytic process in working through these issues contributed considerably to resolving the underlying narcissistic issues and to setting the stage for their more explicit processing" (pp. 459–460). Meissner's formulation suggests that the analysand's increased ability to separate from his mother and recognize that he missed his father made it possible for him to modulate the more blatantly narcissistic elements of his personality. From Meissner's discussion of the case, these developments appear to be more critical to this analysand's modification of his narcissistic orientation than his having worked through the "oedipal ground" and his "ambivalent conflicts."

Meissner says that his analysand manifested many typical narcissistic features. He viewed himself "as special, an exception, as deprived and cheated by fate because his father had died at such an early age, the victim of a sad fate" (p. 457). Meissner points out that this view had been intensified by repeated hospitalizations in the second year of his life because of a severe reaction to antibiotics that resulted in a chronic nephrotic syndrome. His father's sudden death not only was a loss to him but also brought about an alteration of his relationship with his mother, with whom he identified: "For both of them everything was an effort, a demand, a burden. Nothing was right for them; for both, there was little or no engagement or happiness in life. Their common motif was that of suffering, the bearing and finding of burdens everywhere they turned" (p. 448).

Meissner describes in some detail his interventions aimed at helping his analysand modify his narcissism. In the earlier phases Meissner's approach was quite similar to Kohut's, in which he advocated the analyst's mirroring his analysand's grandiosity. Meissner states that he accepted his analysand's view of himself as both "exceptional" and "a victim." His mirroring technique permitted "the contradictory and oppositional aspects of the patient's narcissism [to] come into view. . . . The patient's sense of himself as deprived, burdened, cheated by life, inadequate, inferior, worthless and shameful, came to stand side by side with feelings of specialness, entitlement, privilege, superiority, and his status as 'an exception' " (p. 463). At this stage of the analysis Meissner helped his analysand become aware of and observe these contradictory aspects of his self.

At a later point in the analysis Meissner altered what he called his "interpretative strategy" and was much less accepting of his analysand's claim that he was exceptional as well as a victim:

> The links between the narcissistically inferior and the narcissistically superior configurations are formed in a progressive interpretative process, link by link. In this case, it was a question of the patient gradually coming to see how this sense of entitlement and specialness set the stage for his feelings of deprivation and victimization, and that his feelings of being imposed on, deprived, overwhelmed, and excessively burdened were the result of exaggerated expectations and narcissistic demands. (p. 463)

Meissner was clearly indicating to his analysand that it would be of great benefit to him to recognize that his expectations were unrealistic and modify them. He pointed out to the analysand that his view of himself as a special person inevitably led to great disappointment and to his tendency to deprecate himself. Not unexpectedly, the analysand was reluctant to accept that his expectations were unrealistic:

> Like most narcissistic personalities, my patient would willingly have surrendered his feelings of inferiority, inadequacy, helplessness, impotence, victimization, and depression. But he was reluctant to surrender the sense of himself as entitled and exceptional, as having the right to be taken care of and being given to on his own terms, without any demands being made on him. Nor was he willing to relinquish his wish to be the loved and cherished child who needed to do little beyond existing and pleasing his elders in favor of being a responsible, hard-working adult on whom others could lean. (p. 463)

The analysand's reluctance to make this change took the form of "stoutly insisting that he could have things his way, that the analysis and the analyst should find some way of relieving him of his burdens and his sense of victimization and give him the freedom to satisfy his narcissistic expectations" (p. 464).

When he eventually realized that this too was unrealistic, he became angry; but later it became evident that the analysand was deriving considerable therapeutic benefit from his analysis. Meissner notes that the analysand gradually relinquished "his sense of narcissistic entitlement and specialness" (p. 464). He reported that the improvement became evident in his relationships with members of his family. He became more tolerant and realistic about his mother, his wife, and his son. He recognized that his sense of entitlement created conflict and unhappiness with his wife and began to view her situation with more objectivity and to understand the stresses, anxieties, and difficulties to which she was subjected. He related to her in a less self-centered manner and was more considerate and supportive of her.

Meissner also describes the process through which he established a therapeutic relationship with the analysand. He is cautious in distinguishing between the techniques he used to help the analysand modify his narcissism and those he used to establish the therapeutic relationship. He refers to the latter as "the related process" and maintains that it is the necessary condition for his interpretative strategy to be effective.

Meissner states that in the early stages of the analysis his analysand idealized him and presented himself as "small, insignificant, worthless, inadequate, as a little boy who could do no more than play ineffectively and childishly at the feet of the powerful analyst-father" (p. 465). At the very point when Meissner was encouraging the analysand "to surrender the sense of himself as entitled and exceptional," the analysand was emphasizing his helplessness and his unwillingness to take an active part in modifying his expectations. An analysand who "stoutly insists" on maintaining such a view of himself is clearly unwilling to become engaged in analytic work, whether it be the lifting of repression or the modification of narcissistic expectations. He will want the analyst to take care of him and change the world for him. Under these circumstances the analytic relationship is not a therapeutic one.

Meissner describes his efforts to induce his analysand to become more engaged in the analytic work:

> The analyst does not accept the patient's idealization (acceptance would imply countertransference); he does not endorse or respond to the patient's self-devaluation: by the manner and fact of his interpretation the analyst even lends a degree of respect and acknowledgment to the patient—not of the patient's neurotic view of himself, but to the patient as he is. The implications of the projective process are countered, and the basis is provided for internalization of the analyst's more positive and realistic attitudes into the patient's self-regard. (p. 466)

Meissner used a combination of confrontation and empathy to establish a therapeutic relationship with the analysand. At an earlier phase of the analysis Meissner's goal was to promote his analysand's revelations of his "narcissistic configurations." He states that during that period he "accepted and received unquestioningly" the material his analysand presented to him. But when Meissner discusses how he established a therapeutic relationship with his analysand, he indicates that he did not accept his patient's idealization of him or its counterpart, his devaluation of himself, both of which were associated with his unwillingness to involve himself in the work. This suggests that Meissner substituted a confrontational stance toward his analysand for his original empathic, mirroring one.

Yet Meissner states that he continued to relate to his analysand in an empathic manner. He apparently believed that the empathic aspect of his interactions was more crucial than the confrontational aspect in promoting the analysand's willingness to collaborate with him. Meissner's assertion that he respected his analysand "as he is" suggests that he attempted to communicate to his analysand that he had the potential for making meaningful changes. Apparently, Meissner interacted with his analysand in a manner that aimed at fostering the analysand's internalization of the analyst's values, particularly his belief that it is worthwhile to examine and modify one's behavior and attitudes toward other people. It is clear that Meissner was seeking to promote a process in which the analysand plays an active part. This view stands in contrast to Rothstein's conception of the therapeutic process with severe narcissistic personalities, where the analysand relates passively to an analyst who functions for him as a "narcissistically invested introject." According to Meissner, the analyst does not serve merely to mirror, hold, and contain the analysand. When Meissner indicates his respect and acknowledgment to the analysand "as he is," he is seeking to enhance the analysand's willingness to recognize the extent of his self-deception and to make the active effort to modify his unrealistic expectations. Although he did confront the analysand with his passive attitude about engaging in the work, he did not insist that the analysand admit that he behaved in a self-centered way. Meissner aimed at promoting his analysand's potential for actively participating with him in coming to this realization.

Meissner draws a cautious distinction between those interactions with his analysand that were essential for establishing a therapeutic relationship and those that were associated with his "interpretative strategy" and led to therapeutic changes. From Meissner's material, it is clear that he established a therapeutic relationship through using a combination of confrontation and empathy to evoke the analysand's active involvement. The active analytic work that resulted from Meissner's interpretative strategy was directed toward helping the analysand establish "links between the narcissistically inferior and the narcissistically superior configurations" of his personality. He demonstrated to the analysand that "his sense of entitlement and specialness" preceded "feelings of deprivation and victimization." Meissner speaks of forging the links between these unconnected configurations. This analysand had not become aware of the obvious fact that unrealistic expectations are followed by disappointments. Meissner's approach helped him make this crucial discovery.

A narcissistic individual similar to Meissner's analysand fails to establish many of the links essential for adequate reality-testing. This is because the faulty interactions of his childhood have resulted in the deployment of more global and primitive defenses than repression. He cannot lift repression because he did not deploy it in his childhood. Moreover, his self-centeredness and his lack of awareness of how other people feel and of how they respond to his behavior keeps him from recognizing many of the connections between external events and internal ones. This lack of awareness impedes his relationships with other people. The solipsistic quality of his relationships has interfered with his acquisition of meaningful intermediate links between his own mental states and external events.

There remains the question of whether this beneficial outcome is best accomplished through an empathic or through a confrontational approach. When an analyst interacts with an analysand more empathically than confrontationally, he will tend to accept the links between events the analysand is willing to make by himself. When he interacts more confrontationally, he will tend to insist that the analysand recognize the links the analyst believes to be the significant ones. Meissner's clinical material does not give a clear-cut indication of how he would answer this question. He states that the links between configurations "are forged in a progressive interpretative process, link by link." The word "forge" suggests that the analysand would perceive the analyst as actively persuading him to accept a connection between events. Yet Meissner states that in the case under discussion "it was a question of the patient gradually coming to see" how his sense of entitlement was linked to his feelings of deprivation. The phrase "gradually comes to see" suggests that Meissner intended to allow the analysand to draw his own conclusions about the nature of the links between one state of mind and another. It is likely that he used a mixture of empathy and confrontation in carrying out this interpretative strategy.

In those analytic situations where the analysand has come to realize that his behavior and attitudes are generally acceptable to his analyst, he will become most willing to engage in the analytic work. This is especially the case if he feels his analyst is uncritical of his reluctance to involve himself in the process. However, the analysand's reluctance often becomes intensified when he is faced with the possibility of recognizing distressing links between events of which he had been unaware. An analysand may avoid making a connection between what he calls his assertive behavior and the fact that he alienates others by his actions. He may proclaim that if he were to renounce his assertiveness, he would be reduced to humiliating complacency. In response, his analyst may endeavor to point out that there is a difference between arguing tactfully for what one is entitled to and insisting that others have acted illegitimately. Nonetheless, in spite of this effort to mitigate his resistance, the analysand may continue to refuse to make what for the analyst is an obvious connection.

The issue is whether an analyst who persists in forging a link in the face of an analysand's reluctance to accept the connection will promote or interfere with that analysand's potential for modifying his narcissistic orientation. An analyst who confines his interventions to confronting the analysand with his counterproductive behavior and who insists that he accept the analyst's own conception of events runs the risk of being perceived as a controlling parent. The analysand will feel that the analyst is critical of him and will withdraw from active participation in the analytic work. It is often possible, however, for the analyst to clarify the links between events in a manner that is acceptable to the analysand. This is likely to occur in those situations where the analyst helps the analysand realize the possible beneficial effects of making and accepting a connection between his behavior and others' perception of him. Meissner's empathic interaction with his analysand helped the analysand realize that it was in his best interests to respond empathically to his wife rather than to remain unresponsive to her.

Meissner's analysand presented clinical features similar to those presented by Hanly's. Each manifested a mix of narcissistic and neurotic characteristics. Each responded positively to his analyst's eventual acknowledgment of his efforts to work in the analysis. Yet Hanly's analysand was capable of lifting repression because her dialogues with her parents had fostered the deployment of repression as the primary defense.

It is not clear whether Meissner's analysand had sufficiently helpful dialogues in his childhood for him to have used repression as a major defense. Meissner asserts that his analysand did lift repression, but I do not believe that Meissner's clinical material provides sufficient evidence that this lifting occurred. Meissner's useful emphasis on his approach to his analysand's narcissistic orientation obscures this important issue. The analysand had come to realize that his lack of sensitivity to his wife's feelings was responsible for their conflict and unhappiness and became capable of behaving toward her in a less self-centered manner. Yet it is not apparent whether if his analysis had continued he would have been able to pay attention and accept responsibility for his angry and sadistic wishes toward her.

6 The Uses of Fantasy in the Analytic Dialogue

There is a correlation between the nature of the dialogues a child has with his parents during his pre-oedipal and oedipal periods and the type of defenses he subsequently employs. A child makes use of the sophisticated and selective mechanism of repression in those situations where a generally available parent has helped him make sense out of manifestations of the instinctual conflicts that become apparent during his oedipal period. The child will manifest more primitive defenses than repression in those situations where generally unavailable parents relate to him in an unhelpful way. This parental failure causes the child to use the global mechanisms of denial and projection and, subsequently, to develop a narcissistic orientation. Someone who has found it necessary to make use of primitive modes of defense is unlikely to respond progressively to a classical analytic approach aimed at lifting repression. In that case the analytic stalemate that has developed may be ameliorated when the analyst shifts to another approach.

It is often difficult, however, for the analyst to decide whether the analysand would be better served by his altering the way he implements the classical approach or by shifting to another approach. Many analysands manifest both neurotic features and a fairly well developed narcissistic orientation. In some instances it is hard to determine to what extent the analysand has used repression in addition to his more obvious defenses. In chapter 5 I posed the question of whether a continuation of the analysis Meissner was conducting would have promoted his analysand's capacity to lift repression. The analysand had been greatly helped by his analytic experience; at the time the analysis terminated, he was considerably more realistic and more empathic toward his wife and family. But the case does not allow a definite conclusion as to whether the analysand had the potential to lift repression and the ability to experience and tolerate archaic aspects of his instinctual wishes.

An analyst who is presented with a clinical picture similar to the one Meissner describes should try to evaluate the quality of his analysand's early dialogues with his parents. If he considers it likely that those dialogues were helpful ones, he should continue to implement a classical approach. In those instances when he cannot arrive at a clear-cut conclusion, he will have to decide whether the analytic process itself can compensate for the relative failure of the parents and whether the analytic dialogue can promote the analysand's willingness to pay attention to and assume responsibility for his instinctual wishes if the analysand appears to be more narcissistic than neurotic. A closer examination of the nature of the childhood dialogues should be of value in determining this issue.

Dialogue is integrally involved in the process of repression. When a child employs repression as a primary defense, we can only assume that a parent has responded in helpful ways to the child's uttered concerns about the threatening aspects of his instinctual wishes. This parent must eventually forbid the expression of the more primitive aspects of the child's instinctual wishes, but at the same time he or she will have offered the child a verbal context for those feelings that he has acknowledged.

The parent will have used language in a manner that helps the child experience his libidinal and aggressive wishes. Sooner or later the connotations of the child's wishes will make it necessary for him to turn his attention away from their more threatening aspects. Nonetheless, the fact that his parent has encouraged rather than discouraged his speaking about his mental experiences will enhance his potential for talking about his emotional states. He has been helped to elaborate his feelings in a linguistic form and to communicate what he has elaborated to another person.

A fundamental way a child has of putting his feelings into language is through the creation of a fantasy. The process of fantasizing, like the process of repression, is usually considered from an intrapsychic perspective. Freud viewed a fantasy as a wish-fulfilling product of the imagination.[1] Joseph Sandler recalls Freud's postulation that fantasizing does not occur until the development of the reality principle.[2] The person who imagines a gratifying situation remains aware of reality even as he compensates for its frustrations. Hence from this perspective fantasizing is a highly developed function of the ego.

Yet it is essential to consider the process of fantasizing from an interpersonal as well as an intrapsychic point of view. Many of the frustrations for which the use of a fantasy compensates are secondary to another person's unavailability. More significantly, someone often relates his fantasy to another person to make an indirect statement or to ask an indirect question. This allusive mode of communicating is particularly common in childhood. As I have emphasized, the parent's sensitivity and alertness to the child's latent message will influence the child's subsequent willingness and ability to use language to communi-

1. Sigmund Freud (1911), Formulations on the Two Principles of Mental Functions, *S.E.* 12, pp. 213–226.

2. Joseph Sandler and Humberto Nagira (1963), Aspects of the Metapsychology of Fantasy, *Psychoanalytic Study of the Child* 18, pp. 159–194.

cate what he is feeling. Consequently, the nature of the parental response will have a basic effect on the child's ability to employ repression rather than more primitive defenses.

There are events that occur during the course of a child's development, such as the birth of a sibling, that evoke intense feelings of desire and anger in him. On such occasions the parent's response to a fantasy that the child relates to express his concern about what he is experiencing is critical to determining his defenses. At the time he reveals his fantasy to his parent, the child is already threatened by the implications of the event as well as by the feelings he has developed in reaction to it. In the case of the birth of a sibling, the child realizes that the new child will receive a considerable part of his mother's attention and love, which had previously been given entirely to him. At the same time he is concerned that his jealousy toward his sibling as well as his anger toward his mother for having betrayed him will alienate her. The child has a double purpose in relating his fantasy to his mother. He is attempting to persuade her to resume their relationship as it had existed before the arrival of the sibling. He is also trying to discover whether the anger he feels toward his mother because of her refusal to accede to his request has impaired her love for him. The child feels that his relationship with his mother is seriously threatened and seeks a means to reconstitute it in the face of his anger.

Under these circumstances it is sometimes possible for a mother to respond to the report of her child's fantasy in a way that reassures him that she not only cares for him but is interested in promoting his understanding of what he is experiencing. Her response may help the child realize that she is available to help him make sense out of what he is feeling even though she cannot respond to the request he has indirectly expressed in his fantasy. When this occurs, a kind of rapprochement takes place. The new event in the child's life has jeopardized his relationship with his mother; he has dared to defy her and has tried to persuade her to change her behavior. Yet he is searching for evidence that in spite of his rebellious attitude, she will continue to love him and to help him cope with his reactions to the new event in his life.

Interchanges of this nature during childhood promote the potential for lifting repression in the analytic situation. In chapter 1 I discussed the little boy who told his mother a story about losing his unborn sibling in the woods. This is one instance of the various ways a child develops the potential for lifting repression. His mother did not criticize him for his anger at his sibling but rather shared with him similar feelings she had had in her childhood toward her siblings. The boy's relationship with his mother was threatened by his anger at her for having had another child. His purpose in relating his story to her was to persuade her not to have that child. His mother's empathic and uncritical attitude toward his request and her willingness to indicate to him that she herself had similar angry feelings is the prototype of the rapprochement I am referring to. His relationship with his mother was jeopardized by his unrequited love, and he angrily left her for a "walk in the woods." He returned from this fantasized walk without his sibling to ascertain from his mother whether it would be possible to reestablish a meaningful relationship with her. Her response was intended to show that she retained her love for him and was ready to share with him the experiences he was going through.

It has been increasingly obvious to me that a markedly narcissistic individual does not have this type of dialogue with a parent during his childhood. Both of the mothers Rothstein (1982) discusses in his case material behaved toward their children in ways that precluded a rapprochement. Of course, there are parents who are more available and interested in their child's welfare than the mothers Rothstein describes. Yet parents frequently fail to recognize that when their child reports a fantasy, he is attempting to make sense out of his feelings or persuade them to change their behavior. The child is then likely to believe that it is pointless to expect his parents to respond helpfully if he were to solicit their assistance, and he will keep his fantasies to himself.

It should be noted that most persons, even those who appear to be quite narcissistic, have had some type of interaction, however flawed, with their parents in which they effect a reconciliation after a breach in their relationship has occurred. On occasion the interchanges leading to the reconciliation may even have the features of the rapprochement. But usually the narcissistic individual will have found it necessary to appear to agree with his parent's version of reality as a price for restored harmony. He will not have the good fortune of sensing that his parent respects his autonomy and wishes to promote his understanding. Under these circumstances the child, like those described by Winnicott, will present a "false self" to his parent. He overtly accedes to his parent's demands while keeping to himself his feelings about the conditions the parent has set for reestablishing their relationship.

Even after a long analysis, it may not be possible for the analyst to determine the extent to which a narcissistic analysand's parents have responded to the latent message in the fantasies he reported to them. Judging from what many narcissistic analysands report about their childhood interactions, as well as from how they interact in the analytic situation, such a rapprochement took place only rarely. This raises the question of whether the narcissistic analysand is able to engage in the kind of analytic work that eventuates in his reporting his fantasies to his analyst and thereby promotes his potential for paying attention to and assuming responsibility for his instinctual wishes. By contrast, the neurotic analysand, who has benefited from his childhood dialogues, is much more capable of lifting the repression of his instinctual wishes, which are expressed in the fantasies that he reports in the analytic situation.

The neurotic analysand's aim in relating his fantasies to his analyst changes over time. A closer examination of this process provides the means for evaluating whether a narcissist can likewise make use of his fantasies to achieve insight into his instinctual wishes.

The neurotic uses his fantasies both to compensate for a state of intrapsychic distress and to influence the behavior of those he considers to have contributed to that distress. When the neurotic experiences anxiety or guilt or feels frustrated over some aspect of his instinctual wishes, he is likely to imagine another interaction in which his wish will be satisfied and in which he will avoid feeling anxious or guilty. More significantly, he may relate the fantasy he has elaborated to another person in order to alter the way that person behaves. The nature of the analysand's request or demand, which is conveyed in the fantasy, may vary considerably and will change as the analysis progresses. Early in the analysis the analysand may seek to elicit more direct manifestations of love, support, and sympathy from the analyst. He may also try to find out how his analyst actually feels about him. As the analysis progresses, the analysand may employ his fantasies to clarify or ascertain what the analyst expects him to accomplish. He may use his fantasies to express his concerns about becoming involved in the analytic work. Eventually he may offer his fantasies to the analyst as a means of inquiring whether they accurately represent aspects of the repressed wishes he has been encouraged to observe.

The neurotic analysand, with the potential for lifting repression, initially presents the products of his imagination, particularly fantasies, to persuade the analyst to act in a more gratifying manner toward him. When he realizes that the analyst is not going to alter his behavior, he may become angry. Nonetheless, he is capable of recognizing that the analyst is responding to his attempt to influence him in a nonjudgmental, uncritical, and helpful manner. Sooner or later the analysand will appreciate the fact that even though the analyst does not offer direct gratification, he is willing to offer help in furthering his understanding of himself. At that point the analysand begins to collaborate with the analyst in lifting his repression, and a rapprochement is achieved.

This process is best illustrated by material from the analysis of an analysand who appeared to have more neurotic issues than narcissistic ones. Many of his early dialogues with his parents, especially those with his mother, seem to have been healthy, thereby allowing him to employ repression as his major defense. He was actively aware of what other people were experiencing and how his behavior affected them. He was capable of listening to and reflecting on what his analyst pointed out to him.

The analysand had raised strong defenses against experiencing and expressing his anger. For several years his analyst had been encouraging him to become more aware of the anger he felt toward significant people in his life, including the analyst. By the time this episode occurred, he had come to realize what it was that the analyst expected him to accomplish but remained reluctant to pay attention to and acknowledge his negative feelings. During one session he elaborated a hypothetical situation in which he described himself as being mistreated by someone with whom he was working. He then asked the analyst whether he would be justified in expressing his annoyance directly to his coworker. The analyst did not answer his question, nor did he interpret the transference significance of the material. He confined his activity to encouraging the analysand to continue his associations.

The next day the analysand reported that as he approached the analyst's office, he had the fantasy of being followed by a group of angry, shouting men who were raising their fists and stamping their feet. The analyst told the analysand that he apparently had not realized how angry he was at the analyst.

In response, the analysand revealed that he had felt angry at the analyst the previous day after he had not answered his question, and he said that this was the first time he had actually felt angry at the analyst. He acknowledged that he had wavered between reporting and concealing his angry reaction. Though he realized that this was the type of reaction the analyst had been encouraging him to observe, he was concerned about how the analyst would react to his anger. Before coming to the session, he had decided not to acknowledge that he had been angry. But once the analyst commented on his fantasy about the angry men, he realized that his anger had persisted.

These circumstances suggest that the analysand elaborated and reported his fantasy in an effort to reestablish a relationship with his analyst. The relationship had been stressed as a result of the analyst's withholding behavior during the previous session. After the analysand had decided it was unsafe for him to tell the analyst directly that he was angry at him, he created a fantasy in which that anger was expressed in a displaced form. By reporting the fantasy to the analyst, he was seeking to determine how the analyst would respond and whether he would help him understand the significance of the feelings he had elaborated into the fantasy. The analyst's benign response obviously indicated that he was still available to further his analysand's understanding of what he was experiencing. A rapprochement had occurred, and the therapeutic aspects of the analytic relationship had been strengthened.

By contrast, the narcissistic individual has had few, if any, helpful childhood dialogues, and he is not likely to have participated in a rapprochement of this nature. Someone whose parents have been generally unavailable and unresponsive will not persist in his efforts to persuade them to alter their behavior or elicit their help in furthering his understanding of what he is experiencing. His sense of well-being impaired by his parents' unavailability, he elaborates his fantasies to restore his self-esteem rather than to compensate for the frustration of his instinctual wishes. Unlike the neurotic, who anticipates that other people would respond in a helpful manner if he were to reveal the products of his imagination to them, the narcissist uses his fantasies to sustain himself. In the analytic situation he will report his fantasies and dreams out of a desire to comply with what he believes the analyst expects him to do rather than out of a desire to elicit gratification or help from him. The analytic dialogue that occurs when a narcissistic analysand reports fantasies to his analyst is less likely to lead to the lifting of repression than one that takes place between a neurotic analysand and his analyst. This distinction becomes increasingly problematic, however, when an analyst is confronted with an analysand who, while appearing to be narcissistic, begins to employ fantasies in ways similar to those of the neurotic.

During the course of a long analysis, a narcissistic analysand's purpose in elaborating and reporting his fantasies to his analyst was modified in a distinctly neurotic fashion. Ultimately, he appeared to create fantasies to elicit his analyst's help in achieving an understanding of what he was experiencing. Even though the analysand did not lift the repression of the more archaic aspects of his desire and anger, he did become aware of the intensity of his longing for his father and for paternal responses from the analyst and of his anger when he believed that his wish was not fulfilled. It was difficult for the analyst to decide whether this favorable development reflected the presence of unsuspected helpful childhood dialogues or was the result of helpful dialogues in the analytic situation.

In the fifth year of difficult analytic work, an analysand reported a fantasy he had had on the way to the analyst's office. This fantasy was unlike ones he had told his analyst previously. On this occasion he had elaborated his angry and sadistic feelings into a coherent narrative. Previously his elaborated fantasies reflected his grandiosity but were devoid of aggressive and competitive components. Early in the analysis, when he experienced angry feelings, he would become anxious but would confine the manifestations of his anger to fleeting visual images of someone hurting him or of himself hurting another person. There were, however, no organized linguistic components in the fantasies he reported. In the fantasy he now described, he indicated that a woman toward whom he had had a slight interest had been raped and brutally murdered in a distant city. He pictured himself traveling to where this attack had taken place and systematically and violently exterminating the murderers. He also portrayed himself as seeking out the policemen who he believed had allowed the woman's death to occur, in order to blind them for their apparent complicity in the crime. He stated that he had experienced considerable pleasure while having this fantasy. He acknowledged that he felt somewhat embarrassed while reporting the fantasy to the analyst because of what he termed its "gruesome features." This change in the characteristics of his fantasies was an indication of an increased ability to sustain himself and to make use of his imagination on those occasions when his sadistic feelings began to emerge into consciousness.

The analysand had well-defined narcissistic aspects to his personality. He was self-centered and somewhat grandiose. He often behaved in an unrealistic manner, unmindful of the consequences of his behavior for himself and its effects on other people. Though he had many good male friends who were devoted to him and concerned about him, he had not found it possible to establish a prolonged, intimate relationship with a woman. He had been married twice, but both marriages were tumultuous and ended in divorce. He also had a number of neurotic symptoms. He became very anxious in the presence of aloof, attractive women and was phobic about being alone in his house. During the first phase of his analysis he was unaware of any connection between his sexual and aggressive wishes and his symptoms.

The analysand's mother appeared to be devoted to him,

taking great pleasure in his successes and often praising him inordinately. He had been very attentive to her during his childhood. In adolescence, however, he gradually came to realize that her praise and approval were conditional. He recognized that she was quite controlling and that she would belittle any effort he made to move away from her. He recalled several occasions during his childhood and adolescence in which he became enraged at her.

It was difficult to ascertain to what extent his anger toward his mother arose from his sense that she rejected his love and to what extent it derived from his reaction to her controlling behavior. During his adolescence, when he began to devalue her, he focused on her lack of intelligence and her rigidity. His need to devalue her persisted into his adult life and continued, although with less severity, throughout his analysis.

The analysand's father was a hard-working man who was actively involved with his family. Though his father cared for and was concerned about his son, he generally concealed his positive feelings and treated the young man in a brusque manner, rarely praising and often criticizing him. When the analysand turned to him for help, his father responded ungrudgingly but offered his advice in a dogmatic, devaluing manner and did not tolerate any dissension. As a result, the analysand stopped listening to what his father said to him. In the course of his analysis he discovered that he had longed for his father's approval.

The nature of his early dialogues with his parents could not be determined with any certainty. His early relationship with his mother was close, and he experienced intense desire for her. Her strong need to fit him into her image of what he should be suggests that she would not have tried to help him modulate his libidinal and aggressive feelings. His father was concerned about the analysand's tendency to act in self-damaging ways. However, the dogmatic and far from empathic way his father offered his help precluded the analysand's paying attention to him.

Initially the analysand appeared to have a limited capacity for observing himself. He had great difficulty in tolerating and understanding his feelings, particularly his angry ones, and was vague about the nature of the analytic work involved in lifting repression. In fact, he seemed determined not to relinquish his self-centered view of events. He would report dreams and fantasies that apparently referred to aspects of his relationship with his analyst, yet he would act as if he were helpless when called on to associate. He sometimes would ask the analyst what he thought his associations "meant." Not infrequently, when the analyst offered a "meaning" for them, he would deprecate his suggestion. On other occasions he would respond to an interpretation by indicating that he was crestfallen because he had not recognized the significance of the dream or fantasy by himself. This interaction was a replication of the way he had responded to his father's advice. When this similarity was pointed out to the analysand, he became somewhat more capable of listening to the analyst. However, he continued to be unwilling, or unable, to pay attention to the competitive, dependent, or homosexual feelings manifest in his dreams and associations.

In addition to his attempts to help the analysand lift repression, the analyst directed considerable therapeutic work toward helping him understand why he was having difficulty in becoming intimate with a woman. During the first several years of his analysis he showed a marked tendency to find fault with and devalue women. In this respect his behavior was reminiscent of the way he treated his mother. Women did become interested in him and would indicate that they cared for him. Yet sooner or later his critical and withholding behavior would alienate them, and they would terminate the relationship. During the early phases of his analysis he had been largely unaware of the effect his self-centered behavior had on women. But by the time he reported the fantasy I have described, he had come to understand that his egocentric actions and attitudes were detrimental to his relationships with them. Moreover, he had come to recognize that he often became angry when he felt a woman was not paying sufficient attention to him or was placing what he considered to be unrealistic demands on him. His more realistic understanding of why he tended to devalue and antagonize women led to an improvement in his interactions with them. Nonetheless, he avoided establishing a protracted, intimate relationship.

It is likely that the analysand was able to acquire this understanding because his analyst discussed his devaluation and criticism of women in a nonjudgmental manner. Although the analyst highlighted the effect the analysand's actions had on women, the analysand felt that in general these clarifications were in his best interest and of help to him. The analysand stated that he could distinguish between the ways that the analyst and his father would talk about his self-centeredness.

Although at this point in his analysis the analysand was demonstrating improvement in his relations with women, he showed little capacity to understand his feelings about them. His devaluation and criticism of women were more than a manifestation of his narcissistic, self-centered orientation whereby he considered that no woman was good enough for him. They also served to protect him from experiencing the intense feelings that would have developed if he had allowed himself to become more intimate with one. He was able to avoid placing himself in this threatening situation by discovering a flaw in any woman that would justify his withdrawing from her.

The analysand's elaboration of the fantasy I have described represented a change in the way he expressed his anger. Previously he had either become anxious when he started to feel angry, especially toward a woman, or had manifested his anger in the form of transient sadistic and masochistic images. This change suggests that by this point the analytic process had improved the analysand's capacity to sustain himself in situations where he became angry. Even though he had not been able to fix his attention toward these threatening feelings, he was now apparently able to delay responding in an unmediated manner long enough to elaborate derivatives of his angry feelings in the form of a coherent fantasy. The analyst's uncritical attitude toward whatever the analysand was experiencing and his encouragement to observe the various aspects of his anger had modified the analysand's fear and guilt about expressing it. These interactions were probably responsible for his increased ability to elaborate his feelings of anger into a narrative rather than express them in a peremptory way outside of his control.

The analysand's immediate aim in elaborating this fantasy appears to have been to sustain himself in the face of intense feelings whose source he did not recognize. His willingness to report this sustaining fantasy was perhaps reinforced by his sense that the analyst would be pleased with his newfound capacity to use his imagination. In the early part of the session he appeared to be content with just relating the fantasy and did not associate to it. He seemed to be unaware that he himself was the author of a story in which a woman was raped and murdered, portraying himself as outraged by these events. In his fantasy he was the avenger of wrongs committed by other people.

The analyst suggested that the analysand say something more about the woman in the fantasy beyond the fact that she was a slight acquaintance. The analysand then revealed that he had called her up the night before he had the fantasy and that she had not been available for a date at the time he had requested. The analyst asked him to recall how he had felt on this occasion. He acknowledged that he had been quite angry and had thought to himself that she did not have the right to refuse his invitation. He reported that he had told himself he was being unrealistic and grandiose and did not think about her again until he had the fantasy.

The fact that the analysand had made almost no effort to reflect on the significance of his fantasy indicates that his purpose in elaborating it was clearly not to further his understanding of himself. In the fantasy he reported, he acted as if he were justifiably angry at criminals and complacent policemen. He did not recognize that his anger was a reaction to the woman's rejection of him the night before.

The analyst seriously contemplated the possibility that the analysand's fantasy also indicated the struggle he was undergoing about the possibility of expressing his anger at the analyst. The analysand had for some weeks been requesting that the analyst change the time of one of his sessions to an hour more convenient for him. Because of the limitations of his own schedule, the analyst had not acceded to this request.

It is significant that throughout his analysis the analysand had a strong reluctance to allow himself to have well-defined libidinal and aggressive feelings toward the analyst. The analysand had indicated that he was afraid of the consequences of acknowledging his desire for a close relationship with the analyst. He had revealed that from time to time he had felt transient feelings for the analyst during an analytic hour. It was obvious, however, that he would rapidly turn his attention away from these feelings and often could not remember that he had had them just a short time before. On a number of those occasions the analyst had highlighted the fact that the analysand was highly conflicted about experiencing love or anger toward him.

The analyst had remained alert to the possibility that his analysand might have a reaction to the analyst's inability to acquiesce to his request for a change in appointments. Several times before he reported his fantasy the analysand had come very late to the session, and a few times he had missed it altogether. When the analyst suggested that the analysand might be demonstrating his displeasure at the analyst by coming late, the analysand responded by emphasizing the realistic reasons that interfered with his presence at the session, maintaining that he was not angry at the analyst. The analyst had suggested to the analysand that he was perhaps angrier at him than he realized and might be reluctant to express that anger because he was fearful of how the analyst might react to it.

Toward the end of the session in which the analysand had reported his fantasy, the analyst stated to him that the content of his fantasy indicated that he was angry at the woman for refusing to go out with him and that he had manifested his anger in a disguised manner. He pointed out that the analysand had created a fantasy in which a woman was murdered and that he absolved himself of the responsibility for this murder by fantasizing that he had punished those who murdered her. He then suggested that there was a similarity between what had transpired between the analysand and the woman and between the analysand and himself. The analyst then stated that some of the rage the analysand had experienced in the fantasy represented his anger at the analyst for not changing the time of his appointment.

It is clear that the analyst believed that his analysand had elaborated and then reported his fantasy in an attempt to inform the analyst that he was angry at him and persuade him to change the appointment. The analyst concluded that the indirect and allusive manner in which his analysand had expressed his anger in the fantasy indicated that he was concerned about how the analyst would react if he were to express it directly.

It is questionable, however, whether at this point of his analysis the analysand had become conscious enough of his anger at the analyst to accept the analyst's interpretation as meaningful. It is apparent that the anger the analysand elaborated in his fantasy was not being directly expressed toward the analyst. The analysand first displaced his anger from the analyst to a woman and then from her to anonymous murderers. Lawrence Friedman (1984) has suggested that analysands often report clinical material that includes allusions to a wish "to readjust the analyst's place in the world of the patient's desire." It is his view that an analysand may frequently express indirectly and allusively a wish to influence the analyst's behavior. Yet he indicates that this wish may be experienced with varying degrees of consciousness. He describes what he calls "explicit" allusions that refer to the conscious thought an analysand has about influencing the analyst's behavior but that the analysand subsequently decides not to act upon. He draws a distinction between explicit allusions arising out of mental activity that may be recalled with relative ease and implicit allusions occurring at a far less conscious level of mental activity, which, because of their obscurity, are so difficult to decipher that Friedman suggests that they have "implications neither party will ever be aware of." In those instances when the analysand is conscious of his wish, and especially when he can recall deciding not to implement it, he is likely to accept his analyst's interpretation about it.

The fact that the analysand under discussion, in elaborating and reporting his fantasy, had deployed both displacement and projection makes it unlikely that he could recall that he had thought about expressing his anger at the analyst or that he had decided that it would entail too much of a risk for him to do so. The mental activity through which he elaborated his fantasy probably occurred at a less conscious level than the one where "decisions" are usually made.

In response to the analyst's interpretation, the analysand acknowledged that the parallel the analyst had drawn between his anger at the woman and at the analyst seemed plausible. It is not surprising, however, that the analysand continued to maintain that he was unaware of feeling any anger at the analyst beyond a "mild annoyance" for his not meeting the analysand's request.

After this episode the analysand continued to express his anger indirectly at the analyst for a period of two months. He no longer appeared on time to the appointment and then stopped coming to it altogether. He maintained steadfastly that his absence was due to his need to attend to his business. After one of these missed sessions he offered a proposal to the analyst. He stated that he would pay for the missed appointments provided the analyst would hold the hour open until he had made a decision about whether to reclaim it. He indicated that he would make this decision in six months, but for the present he would not come to the appointment.

The analyst was irritated by the analysand's proposal. He felt as though he were being told to wait until the analysand made up his mind about whether it was worth his while to come to the appointment. In an uncharacteristic response the analyst abruptly told the analysand that he would not keep the hour open. He also stated that if after six months the analysand wanted the hour again, they could talk about it at that time.

The analysand's initial reaction to his recognition that the analyst was angry at him was to become anxious. He stated that he had not expected the analyst to become disturbed at his request. He said that in fact he had anticipated that the analyst would be pleased to be paid for not working. He indicated that he believed he was one of the analyst's few patients and that therefore the analyst would not have a problem in keeping an hour open for him. The analyst perceived the thinly disguised devaluation of him in the analysand's explanation for his proposal. Nonetheless, he was able to recover his analytic attitude. He came to the conclusion that it would be in the analysand's best interests if he could acknowledge to the analysand that the proposal had angered him, and he did so. The analysand responded to this acknowledgment by stating that he felt relieved and pleased, for he now saw the analyst as more human and more involved with him than he had previously felt him to be.

Shortly thereafter the analysand reported a dream in which he expressed his anger at the analyst much more explicitly. In this dream he went with a woman to an inn where he had reserved a large suite for the two of them. When he arrived, the manager of the inn told him that the suite was not available and instead gave him a small, undesirable room. After going to this room, he located the original suite and discovered that it had been given away to a "very sexy woman." He became enraged and began to look for the manager to give him "a piece of his mind." He reported that he woke up before he found the manager.

The analysand realized that the innkeeper of his dream represented the analyst. Moreover, he indicated that he himself had become conscious of his anger at the analyst because he had not given him the hour he desired. He also recognized that he intended to devalue the analyst when he had claimed to be one of the analyst's few patients and had implied that the analyst would like to be paid for not working. He did not reject the analyst's suggestion that his devaluation of him was in reaction to his rejection of the analysand's proposal.

Yet the analysand still found it difficult to tolerate his anger toward the analyst, which he had experienced in his dream. Several days later he could not recall the dream, although when the analyst reminded him of it, he was able to recognize it. Nonetheless, over the next two weeks he reported a series of fantasies in which he expressed his rage quite explicitly. On several occasions he fantasized being in a minor traffic accident. In this fantasy the other driver left the scene of the accident, and he set off in pursuit. He reported that when he caught up with the other driver, he criticized him bitterly for the way he had been driving. The analysand stated that he was aware that the anger he had experienced toward the driver was displaced from feelings he had experienced toward the analyst.

About a month later, after the analysand had come ten minutes late to a session, he began by reporting that he had had a new type of fantasy. Before he had this fantasy, he had realized that he was late for the session and had been wondering about how the analyst was feeling about his absence. He went on to state that he had had the fantasy that the analyst was "in anguish." His initial reaction to the fantasy was that he found this notion very exciting, and he relished the idea of telling his fantasy to the analyst when he arrived. But he reported that shortly after having this idea, the thought of revealing his fantasy made him anxious, and he decided to keep it to himself. When the analyst greeted him upon his arrival, the analysand felt that he looked sad. This perception reminded him of his fantasy, and he changed his mind once again about whether to tell it to the analyst. He then concluded that it would be important for him to relate his fantasy and try to understand why he had had it.

The analysand began to associate to his fantasy and to his own tentativeness about disclosing it. He realized that on a number of occasions he had hoped that his father would recognize that he had not displayed affection or appreciation to his son and that he would consequently suffer remorse. The analysand also recalled that he frequently wanted to tell his father that he was sad because of his father's coldness and strictness. He stated that he was afraid to take the steps that might lead to an improvement in their relationship because he believed that his father would rebuff any overture he might make.

The analysand noticed the parallel between these earlier interactions with his father and his behavior and attitude toward the analyst during this episode. As the result of his analyst's clarifications, he had gradually recognized that his passive-aggressive mode of interacting with the analyst and with other people reflected the way he had responded to his father's devaluation of him. Over the next several sessions the analysand realized with increasing vividness that he had often yearned for his father's approval and affection. He stated that he had frequently cried because his father had rarely offered him tangible signs of affection and approval. On a number of occasions during the analytic hour he cried when he recalled his unreciprocated longings for his father's love.

The analysand also revealed that he had become increasingly aware of his wish that the analyst would show signs of affection for him. He remembered that he had cherished those sessions when the analyst had said something the analysand had construed as indicating that the analyst approved of his efforts to accomplish therapeutic work. He began to talk with considerable feeling about his desire to be the analyst's favorite patient. He acknowledged that he was angry at the analyst because the analyst would not offer him a friendship beyond the constraints of a therapeutic relationship.

The analysand's motivation for relating his fantasy to his analyst changed from the time when he had first elaborated it. When the analysand had first considered reporting the fantasy, he was apparently motivated more by a wish to induce an emotional reaction in the analyst and to influence his behavior than by a wish to make use of the analyst's therapeutic help. Immediately after he experienced his perception that the analyst was sad, this balance shifted, and he became significantly more willing to cooperate with the analyst in observing himself.

It is obviously not possible to say with certainty why the analysand had become more willing to pay attention to what he was feeling after he had had the perception that his analyst was sad. This shift occurred at a point in the analysis when he had become aware that the analyst had a genuine interest in helping him understand himself. For a number of years the analyst had been encouraging him to pay attention to his reactions and his feelings. As a result, the analysand had begun to understand what type of analytic work he was expected to accomplish. By the time this episode occurred, the analysand had had ample opportunity to distinguish his analyst's benevolent and noncontrolling attitude toward him from his father's need to impose his will. It should be noted that this episode occurred within two months after the analyst had acknowledged to the analysand that he had reacted angrily to the analysand's proposal that he keep a fifth hour each week open for him. The analysand had stated on several occasions after that earlier episode that he was impressed and moved that the analyst could express anger toward him. The analysand stated that the analyst's behavior on that occasion stood in stark contrast to the way his parents would have responded under similar circumstances.

The present episode took place not long after the analysand had indicated that he realized that the anger he had manifested in his dreams and fantasies towards male figures was displaced from his anger at the analyst. It is apparent that even before this episode occurred, the analysand had become more willing to pay attention to his angry feelings, though he had not as yet recognized that those feelings were secondary to his sense that the analyst did not fulfill his wish for his affection.

A more detailed discussion of the types of responses the analysand was hoping to elicit from the analyst through reporting his fantasy may shed light on the process that led to the analysand's willingness to cooperate with the analyst. The content of the analysand's fantasy suggests that he was expressing the positive as well as negative feelings he was experiencing for the analyst. In elaborating a fantasy in which the analyst was "in anguish," the analysand was clearly imagining a gratifying situation in which he obtained revenge for his analyst's failing to offer him anything more than therapeutic help. But by imagining the analyst to be anguished by his absence, the analysand was expressing a desire for the analyst to love him so much that he would be distressed by the analysand's absence.

When the analysand first considered reporting his fantasy,

he may have been motivated by his positive wishes for the analyst as well as by his negative ones. It is obvious that if the analysand were to inform the analyst that he had thought about making him suffer, he would be attempting to discomfit the analyst. I believe, however, that his act of reporting the fantasy was motivated by more than an unalloyed wish to upset the analyst. In my view, the analysand was hoping to elicit a response from the analyst that might indicate that he cared enough about the analysand to be disconcerted by his absence.

Moreover, the analysand may also have been aware that the analyst wanted him to pay attention to the feelings and wishes that had motivated the elaboration of his fantasy. But the analysand was undoubtedly concerned about the analyst's response if he were to discover that the analysand was experiencing positive and negative feelings for him. The analysand was uncertain whether he could trust his analyst to be helpful or the analyst would change his attitude and become critical of him. It is quite possible that the analysand considered reporting his fantasy as a means of determining whether he could count on the analyst's continued availability after he learned about the nature of his analysand's feelings. The analysand wanted to find out not only whether his analyst cared about him but also whether he cared enough to continue to be available even if he were to discover that the analysand wished to hurt him.

Under these circumstances it is not surprising that the analysand was in fact reluctant to report his fantasy. Only when he reached the analyst's office and had the perception that the analyst was sad did he summon the courage to tell his fantasy and, more significantly, to involve himself in therapeutic work. It is possible that the analysand's perceptions of the analyst's sadness reminded him of the analyst's "humanness," which he had become aware of at the point when the analyst had acknowledged his anger.

Earlier in this chapter I asked whether it is possible for an analysand who has well-defined narcissistic characteristics and has not employed repression as a primary defense to achieve by means of the analytic process the ability to lift the repression of the archaic aspects of his instinctual wishes. The analysand under consideration was self-centered and manifested denial and projection rather than repression as the major way of defending himself from becoming aware of his instinctual wishes. The clinical material I have described indicates that his interactions with his analyst promoted his willingness to acknowledge his desire for the analyst's approval and appreciation as well as to acknowledge his anger at him when he did not reciprocate this desire. Along with this acknowledgment, the analysand recalled similar feelings he had had towards his father while growing up. During the several years prior to these interactions the analysand's sense of his analyst's trustworthiness had been enhanced by the analyst's repeated helpful and nonjudgmental responses toward him. It is also likely that the analyst's willingness to acknowledge his own irritation at the analysand's proposal furthered the analysand's confidence that the analyst would keep the analysand's best interests in mind. These transactions allowed the analysand to distinguish the analyst's generally helpful intentions toward him from his father's openly critical and devaluing behavior. The analysand's conviction that the analyst would maintain a therapeutic and caring stance made it possible for him to observe and risk acknowledging his feelings about the analyst.

There remains the question as to whether this valuable improvement in the way the analysand both observed and communicated his desire and anger to the analyst was associated with a significant change in his willingness to lift the repression of the more archaic aspects of his instinctual wishes. During a long analysis that continued for several years after this series of interactions, the analysand demonstrated only a limited capacity to tolerate his sadism and his death wishes, not to mention his homosexual desires. He continued to express derivatives of these wishes in his dreams and fantasies and acquired an intellectual understanding of their significance. Yet he could rarely tolerate the feelings associated with these wishes long enough to connect them with the events in his life that had evoked them. He developed only a circumscribed ability to accept himself as the agent of his sadism, of his intense wishes to defeat his rivals, and of his homosexuality. When the analysand was outside of the analytic situation, he could recognize that he longed for the analyst's love and that he was angry at him when the analyst appeared to be indifferent to his wishes for closeness. He made little effort, however, when he was by himself to understand the significance of the manifestation of the more archaic elements of his desire and anger toward the analyst.

These considerations suggest that the analysand reported his fantasies, including the fantasy that the analyst was "in anguish," as a means of reality-testing to convince himself of the analyst's benevolent attitude toward him. The analysand had little interest in obtaining the analyst's help in understanding the more walled-off and threatening elements of his instinctual wishes, which were expressed in his fantasies. Of course, once the analysand decided that the analyst would remain helpful if he revealed his feelings, he became clearer about the nature of what he was experiencing. Although he became aware of the circumstances under which it would be safe for him to acknowledge his feelings, he did not deepen his understanding about the more threatening aspects of his wishes.

In chapter 2 I pointed out that Strachey's ([1934] 1969) formulation of the curative process in psychoanalysis emphasizes the importance of the analysand's recognition that in contrast to what he feared, his analyst has benign and helpful intentions toward him. According to Strachey, the analysand will realize that his analyst's behavior and attitude do not warrant the degree of anger he had had toward him. Strachey indicates that this type of reality-testing makes it possible for the analysand to moderate his anger. An analysand will defend himself from experiencing murderous rage at his analyst where he perceives the analyst to be similar to his critical father. He will modulate these archaic manifestations of his anger only after he discovers that by and large his analyst cares about him and will reject only the more imperative aspects of his instinctual wishes.

I have repeatedly suggested that a narcissistic analysand who has had relatively few helpful dialogues with his parents during his childhood is unlikely to have employed repression as his primary defense. He will have little motivation or potential for paying attention to the archaic aspects of his instinctual wishes. Moreover, the limited nature of his early dialogues will have impaired his capacity to test reality and, more particularly, to understand what occurs when he interacts with another person. A favorable analytic situation will provide the opportunity to improve this understanding. Under these conditions the analysand is likely to become more aware of how his behavior affects another person and more sensitive to what someone else may be experiencing. A favorable analytic situation will make it possible for the narcissistic analysand to ascertain that he can safely acknowledge some aspects of his feelings for his analyst.

In my discussion of Strachey's formulation I suggested that when the analysand lifts repression, he does not so much diminish his aggression as experience it more meaningfully. The analysand then considers himself to be the agent of his repressed wishes and accepts responsibility for them. This did not occur in the analysis I have discussed in this chapter, nor is it likely to take place in the analysis of someone with a well-defined narcissistic character. In my view, repression can be lifted only when an analysand's early dialogues with his parents were helpful ones.

Index